# Thoughts of a blind beggar

Also by Gerard Thomas Straub

*The Sun and Moon over Assisi:*
*A Personal Encounter with Francis and Clare*

*When Did I See You Hungry?*

# Thoughts of a blind beggar

## REFLECTIONS FROM A JOURNEY TO GOD

### GERARD THOMAS STRAUB

ORBIS BOOKS

Maryknoll, New York 10545

Founded in 1970, Orbis Books endeavors to publish works that enlighten the mind, nourish the spirit, and challenge the conscience. The publishing arm of the Maryknoll Fathers and Brothers, Orbis seeks to explore the global dimensions of the Christian faith and mission, to invite dialogue with diverse cultures and religious traditions, and to serve the cause of reconciliation and peace. The books published reflect the views of their authors and do not represent the official position of the Maryknoll Society. To learn more about Maryknoll and Orbis Books, please visit our website at www.maryknoll.org.

Library of Congress Cataloging-in-Publication Data
Straub, Gerard Thomas, 1947-
    Thoughts of a blind beggar : reflections from a journey to God / Gerard Thomas Straub.
        p. cm.
    ISBN 978-1-57075-739-6
1. Straub, Gerard Thomas, 1947- 2. Spiritual biography. I. Title.
    BR1725.S77A3 2007
    282.092--dc22
    [B]
                                                      2007013081

"God, have mercy on me in the blindness in which I hope I am seeking you!"

—Thomas Merton
from *Dialogues with Silence*

"We are all beggars. We are all members of a species that is not sufficient unto itself. We are all creatures plagued by unending doubts and restless, unsatisfied hearts. Of all creatures, we are the most incomplete. Our needs are always beyond our capacities, and we only find ourselves when we lose ourselves."

—Johannes Baptist Metz
from *Poverty of Spirit*

"We are a little like the blind man touching the woman he loves, whom he has never seen and never will. The question of the meaning of life, then, is not a full stop at the end of life, but the beginning of a deeper experience of life. It is like a light whose source we cannot see, but in whose illuminations we nevertheless live—whether we delight in its incomprehensible abundance or suffer from its incomprehensible dearth."

—Václav Havel
from *Letters to Olga, June 1979-September 1982*

"The work of the Holy Spirit is that our blind eyes are opened and that thankfully and in thankful self-surrender we recognize and acknowledge that it is so: Amen."

—Karl Barth
from *Church Dogmatics:, The Doctrine of the Word of God*

"I wait, O God, with patience and hope. I wait like a blind man who has been promised the dawning of light."

—Karl Rahner, S.J.
from *Prayers for a Lifetime*

# Contents

Preface *ix*

Prologue: Poverty Road *xv*

A Prefatory Word from St. Bonaventure *xxxii*

1. Vigils *3*

2. Lauds *27*

3. Terce *55*

4. Sext *83*

5. None *111*

6. Vespers *137*

7. Compline *163*

# Preface

"... I think a volume of more or less disconnected thoughts and ideas and aphorisms about the interior life needs no particular apology or excuse. ..."

—Thomas Merton
*New Seeds of Contemplation*

In March of 1995, I found myself seated in an empty church in Rome. I had no idea that an empty church and an empty man were about to become a meeting place of grace. The four-hundred-year-old church was silent. It had been a dozen years since the last time I had spoken to God, and I was not about to break the silence. I was merely resting. But something highly unexpected happened. God broke through the silence. And everything changed. Without warning, I felt the overwhelming Presence of God; I felt immersed in a sea of Love. Within the space of a fleeting moment, I knew—not intellectually, but experientially—that God was real, that God loved me, and that the hunger and thirst I had felt for so long could be satisfied only by God.

In that moment of revelation, I went from being an atheist to being a pilgrim. I went from denying God to searching for God, wanting more than anything else to experience more and more of God. And I also went from being a Hollywood television producer to a documentary filmmaker whose lens is focused almost exclusively on chronic poverty.

This book is the fruit of a long search, a search which is far from over. Over the years, as I pondered the meaning of life and searched for the God who had disappeared from my life, I picked up the habit of jotting down thoughts—tiny epiphanies—which seemed to contain a kernel of truth. Slowly, the kernels matured, blossomed, multiplied, and combined to create a new, larger, deeper outlook on life. My blindness yielded to vision, a vision which at first was weak and opaque, but with each passing day grows stronger.

If you are looking for some orderly pattern or rhyme or reason in the organization of thoughts in this book, you will not find any, for the presentation celebrates randomness. The book is divided into clusters of thoughts; some clusters are very brief and none are more than a page in length. Each cluster is titled. The thoughts were literally scribbled down all around the world and in wildly different environments, whether a busy airport in Amsterdam or a quiet Benedictine monastery snuggled up against a stone wall at the far end of a remote canyon in northern New Mexico. A considerable part of the book was written in the seventeenth-century Franciscan friary of Sant' Isidoro in Rome, Italy. Part of the book was written in the Cistercian monastery of Our Lady of Gethsemani outside Louisville, Kentucky; some of it was written on Thomas Merton's writing table in his secluded hermitage in the woods. Some of it was written in crowded buses in India and at Mother Teresa's home for the dying in Calcutta. Some of this book was written in St. Francis' mountain-top hermitage high above Assisi in Italy; some of it was written at Mount La Verna, at the spot were St. Francis received the Stigmata. Many of the thoughts were scribbled down in the horrific slums of Kenya, Jamaica, Brazil, and the Philippines. A few lines were jotted down in a mosque in Istanbul, Turkey. Parts of the book were written in El Salvador, Mexico, and Canada. Some of it was written in a home for sick children in Chaclacayo, Peru. A great deal of it was written during a half-dozen grace-filled trips to Assisi. Here in the United States, thoughts were jotted down in Philadelphia, Washington, DC, Detroit, Albuquerque, Tucson, San Francisco, San Diego, Tacoma, Cincinnati, Dayton, Cedar Rapids, Raleigh, San Antonio, Orlando, Chicago, and Albany (NY) to name a few American cities which easily spring to mind. Some of it was written at the University of Notre Dame and at St. Bonaventure University in Olean, New York. Each of these far-flung places spoke different things to me about God.

These thoughts chronicle my own spiritual pilgrimage and education, and reflect my personal interest in prayer, poverty, peace, contemplation, compassion, silence, solitude, mercy, sin, and repentance. I suggest reading the book in the order in which it is presented, reading only one or two clusters of thoughts at a time. Go slowly, reflectively, and prayerfully. Once you have gone through it once, the book can be opened randomly again and again whenever you feel the need to spend some quiet time reflecting on any of the book's themes. I pick up the book once or twice a week in order to reconnect to the thoughts which I so easily forget; the repetition helps me see new and deeper meaning in the morsels of truth I discovered along my personal journey to God.

While writing this book, I was graced with the opportunity to spend time in a Cistercian monastery in Kentucky and in a Benedictine monastery in New Mexico. In both places, the monks punctuate their day with seven formal periods of communal prayer, beginning in the middle of the night. *Vigils, lauds, terce, sext, none, vespers,* and *compline* are Latin words designating the seven "hours" of the Liturgy of the Hours, which is the official prayer of the Catholic Church, prayed daily by priests, monks, and nuns all around the world. St. Benedict, in his rule for monks, calls the seven "hours" of prayer the "work of God," or "opus Dei." The monks in these monasteries still come together in prayer seven times a day to praise, thank, and petition God as a community, and to help foster an atmosphere of prayer throughout the day. None of the "hours" actually lasts an hour; all seven add to a little less than three hours of actual time.

St. Francis of Assisi was passionately devoted to the Liturgy of the Hours. While I was writing *The Sun and Moon over Assisi,* the Liturgy of the Hours became a vital part of my personal prayer life, and so I decided to divide this book into seven parts, each named for one of the daily "hours" of prayer. Your daily reading can, of course, be done at any hour of the day or night. Think of the seven "hours" of this book as punctuating an extended period of time, and not a specific day. The book is a pilgrimage back to God during which we pause at least once a day to reflect on our spiritual journey.

St. Francis used to walk the streets of Assisi with a bowl in his hand, going door to door begging for food. An empty beggar's bowl is an apt metaphor for the receptivity and acceptance required in our relationship with God. An ancient Chinese script says, "Come before the divine with a bowl, an empty bowl, a beggar's bowl." Knowing only God could give him what he truly needed, St. Francis went to God with empty hands, divesting himself of all vestiges of self-will and self-interest in order to be fully receptive to God alone. In the wake of the barbaric events of September 11, 2001, and the war in Iraq, beginning in 2003, it is abundantly clear that we are all blind beggars, and we all need to stretch out open hands to God, who will give us sight and teach us how to see things differently, how to see things as they are, in their fullness, wholeness, and connectedness.

Gerard Thomas Straub, SFO
The Feast of St. Clare of Assisi
August 11, 2006
North Hollywood, California

# Poverty Road

Thomas Merton saw the spiritual journey as a metaphorical "going forth into strange countries." For Merton, even going nowhere required travel. Day by day, our entire lives are a journey, a journey to nowhere, a journey to God. I've been around the world, traveled to many "strange countries" in order to get nowhere, in order to arrive at an empty place within me where the fullness of life is hidden.

This prologue tells the story of a journey, an improbable journey. It's a story of a journey from the glamour of Hollywood to the horrors of the worst slums on earth. It's a story of a journey from unbelief to belief, a story of going from riches to rags . . . and being happy about it. It's my story.

I once was a Hollywood television producer and a committed atheist. But those days are now a distant memory. My encounter with St. Francis of Assisi changed my life. My journey with St. Francis has taken me to places I never imagined going. I've lived with the poor in India, Kenya, Brazil, Peru, El Salvador, Mexico, Jamaica, and the Philippines. As I traveled, I was stunned to learn that malnutrition causes the deaths of over six million children every year. And that more than a billion people lack safe drinking water. And half of humanity must survive on the equivalent of two dollars a day.

The horrors of the sprawling slums in those far-away places often brought me to tears. Naked kids being bathed in the streets with water laced with bacteria. Entire families squeezed into one room without electricity or a toilet. The stench of open sewers was nauseating. I was haunted by the massive garbage dumps in the Philippines, where people live, scavenging like vultures through the rotting waste of others. I was shocked by the sight of hundreds of people with leprosy in a leper colony in the Amazon, people with mutilated faces, whose arms and legs had been eaten away by a vile disease I assumed had been eradicated long ago. I was saddened by the suffering in a home in Chaclacayo, Peru, where a saintly American doctor cares for fifty destitute kids with every disease imaginable. While filming a malnourished infant, I became sick to my stomach.

Yet to my amazement, I liked being with the poor. The poor were teaching me about my own poverty, my own weakness. In all those distant places, I learned a lot about poverty and prayer, and the beautiful mystery of life and death.

But I didn't have to leave America to feel the pain of crippling poverty. In this country, 700,000 people are without shelter each night. I filmed for six months in

Skid Row in downtown Los Angeles, where 11,000 homeless people struggle for survival in the shadow of astounding affluence. Every day I witnessed an endless parade of misery, pain, rejection, and loneliness. People slept in cardboard boxes, under tarps or in small tents. Every night in Skid Row more than 700 children are without shelter, forced to share space with the mentally ill and drug addicts. In December of 2005, I spent two weeks in one of the worst slums in America, the Kensington section of Philadelphia, making a second film about the St. Francis Inn, a soup kitchen run by Franciscan friars. Known as "The Badlands," Kensington is a dark, brooding, depressed area where poverty, pain, and drugs thrive. The mean streets of Kensington are littered with throw-away people, people who are marginalized, ignored and forgotten, people whose lives are lived in fear, in overwhelming want, and without hope. It is a place of death and despondency. I spent part of a night in an abandoned building with a homeless man. The temperature was 10 degrees. The windows were broken and the wind howled through the empty, litter-strewn rooms. It snowed through the porous roof. The man was afraid to fall asleep fearing a rat would crawl into his mouth seeking warmth. It was a nightmare. In June of 2006, I filmed another homeless man living in a burned-out abandoned building in Detroit, and he too spoke of his fear of rats.

Yet despite all my time among the poor I am not an expert on poverty. I'm a simple storyteller whose only desire is to communicate the pain and suffering of those locked in the prison of chronic poverty. As I travel the country speaking and showing my films at universities and churches, I tell my audience they have a responsibility to help ease the pain of chronic poverty. I also share the story of how I went from the soap opera tale of "Luke and Laura" on the run to running a non-profit foundation that tries to put the power of film at the service of the poor.

For years, I produced soap operas on all three major networks, including the wildly popular *General Hospital* on ABC. I was a big success. I had a glamorous job. I made tons of money. But something was missing. I had this emptiness inside of me. I tried to fill it with all kinds of things. Mostly bad things. But the emptiness would not go away…because, as I was to discover, the emptiness could only be filled by God. God was what was missing in my life. But because of my power, prestige and money I felt no need for God. My story is about how a saint from medieval Italy walked into the life of a modern, skeptical American and turned it upside down—or more correctly, turned it right side up.

After graduation from a Catholic high school in 1964, I landed a four-week, summer job at CBS in New York. That fall, the Beatles were appearing on the Ed Sullivan Show. CBS had received sacks of mail requesting tickets. My job was to answer all that mail. I completed the task in two weeks, and was told I didn't need to come in for the last two weeks but I'd be paid for them anyway. Not come in? CBS was the most exciting place I'd ever been. As long as I had an ID badge good for two more weeks, I showed up every day, walking the corridors, poking my head into the studios, marveling at the cameras, lights, and sets. It was a magical world that captivated my imagination.

One day, a man spotted me wandering the halls and asked, "Hey, kid . . . are you lost?" I told him I completed my four-week job in half the time and that I was using the balance of the time exploring this exciting place. Two days later, he spotted me again and said, "Hey kid . . . do you want a real job?"

To my parent's horror, I jumped at the chance of getting a lowly clerical job at a television studio rather than going to college. I'm not saying it was a smart thing to do. It was crazy—crazy, but fortuitous, as I was later selected for an executive training program. I was given a new job every three months. By the time I was 21, I was an executive at the CBS Television Network in New York. Television became by life.

By the time I was 35, I had produced the most popular soap on the air: *General Hospital.* And I was the executive producer of an NBC soap opera taped at Rockefeller Center in NYC. I was very successful yet unsatisfied. I was surrounded by people with lots of money and lots of unhappiness. Money and power are addictive and hard to walk away from.

One day, a vice-president of NBC called me into his office and said: "Do you know what your problem is?"

"No," I said, "but I'm sure you're going to tell me."

"Your problem," he said, "is that you think you're an artist. But the thing is we don't want art . . . we want filler to keep the commercials from bumping into each other."

Of course, I knew TV was all about the commercials. And the commercials were about creating desires by convincing us that we need products to make us happy or more sexy. What the vice president meant was that economics were more important than Art. My soap opera could be replaced by a game show that could be produced at a fraction of the cost and still garner the same profit. I vividly recall sitting in my office watching an episode of the show and thinking, "Who would watch this garbage?" To be honest, I never could have mustered the courage to walk away from the garbage. Mercifully, the show was cancelled, and replaced with a game show.

Armed only with a desire to write, I set out on a journey to discover if there was a deeper meaning to life. I spent about three years writing a dark, depressing novel about a man who had become so exhausted from his search for God that he elected to kill himself. The book was an angry scream at the Church. Critics called it a philosophical novel . . . which meant no one bought it. It sold about 300 copies, 50 of which I purchased.

My next book sought to explore the connection between creativity and spirituality. Entitled *The Canvas of the Soul,* the novel's protagonist was an unpublished writer obsessed with the lives of Vincent van Gogh and St. Francis of Assisi. I was more interested in Vincent than Francis, because no artist so thoroughly documented the creative process as did Vincent in a series of letters to his brother Theo. Francis on the other hand was just a pious fairy tale from the Middle Ages who had nothing to say to my modern, skeptical, secular life.

After nearly two years of work, I was hopelessly stuck and reaching the point where I had to abandon my literary dream and return to the Hollywood dream factory and crank out more mindless soap operas that pandered to the most sordid of human desires. Before throwing in the literary towel, I decided to make one more stab at finishing *The Canvas of the Soul.* I thought that visiting Arles in the south of France where Vincent had his most creative years and Francis' home town of Assisi in Italy and walking where the artist and the saint had walked would inspire me to finish.

During my long years away from God and the Catholic Church, I had remained friends with a Franciscan friar who always accepted my unbelief, always made time to talk with me. I asked him if he knew where I could stay in Rome and Assisi. He called the guardian of the friary at Collegio Sant' Isidoro, a 400-year-old seminary operated by friars from Ireland, and I was given the rare privilege of being allowed to stay there for a week.

I arrived at the gate of the friary one morning in March of 1995. A woman working in the office escorted me to my tiny, spartan room. She said I could join the friars for dinner, but the day was mine to wander the vibrant streets of Rome. So, I headed out, excited to see the ancient city. As I walked past a door leading to the church, a beautiful statue caught my eye. I entered the church, but not to pray. I simply wanted to look around. Before hitting the noisy, hot streets, I decided to sit and rest for a while in the quiet, cool church.

An empty church and an empty man became a meeting place of grace. As I rested in the silence something happened, something highly unexpected: *God broke through the silence,* and everything changed. In the womb of the dark church, I picked up a copy of the Liturgy of the Hours and opened it randomly to Psalm 63. In bold face above the psalm it said: "A soul thirsting for God." As I read the words of the Psalm my soul leapt with joy:

> *God, you are my God, I am seeking you,*
> *my soul is thirsting for you,*
> *my flesh is longing for you,*
> *a land parched, weary and waterless;*
> *I long to gaze on you in the Sanctuary,*
> *and to see your power and glory.*
> *Your love is better than life itself,*
> *my lips will recite your praise;*
> *all my life I will bless you,*
> *in your name lift up my hands;*
> *my soul will feast most richly,*
> *on my lips a song of joy, in my mouth praise.*

Without warning, I felt the overwhelming Presence of God. I didn't see any images or hear any words. What I felt was beyond images and words. I felt immersed in a sea of Love. I knew—not intellectually, but experientially—that God was real, that God loved me, and that the hunger and thirst I had felt for so long could only be satisfied by God. In that moment of revelation, I was trans-

formed from an atheist into a pilgrim. I went from deny-
ing God to wanting to experience more of God.

I adopted St. Francis as my spiritual guide. Day-by-
day, this medieval saint showed a modern skeptic how to
enter the heart of God. Over the years, the hillside town
of Assisi became my spiritual home and opened the mys-
tical windows of my soul.

All the friars at Sant' Isidoro were very welcoming. I
tried to enter their daily routine, attending morning and
evening prayers and the daily celebration of the
Eucharist. But my participation was passive. I hadn't
been part of the Church for at least fifteen years. One
evening, the guardian asked me if I wanted to talk. We
had a three-hour period of prayer and reconciliation. It
was both intense and liberating. We ended up by kneel-
ing and praying together in the empty church. The next
day I received the Eucharist.

In the span of a few days, in a place far from home,
the direction of my life changed.

One of the friars was studying at the Pontifical
Gregorian University. The school was founded by St.
Ignatius Loyola and its alumni include more than twen-
ty canonized saints. The friar convinced the Jesuit priest
who headed the communications department to invite
me to visit a class where the students could question a
Hollywood producer. That led to my being invited to
return to the school in the fall to teach a two-week course
on creative writing for film and television.

When I returned in September of 1995, the depart-
ment head asked to see my syllabus. I gave him a blank
stare. He asked again. More silence. I could see it dawn-
ing on his face that I had no idea what a syllabus was.
Again he asked, this time more agitated, "Where is your
syllabus . . . you know, your course outline, what you
expect to do every hour of the 40-hour course."

I shrugged and said, "I don't have a syllabus."

A look of horror crossed his face, and he said, "Well . . . what are you going to do every day?"

I said, plainly and truthfully, "I'm just going to make it up as I go."

He looked at me as if I had two heads and said, "I'm sorry, but that's a little too Franciscan for us."

He assigned a young Jesuit seminarian to help me write a syllabus.

I overcame that rather shaky beginning and was invited back four more times, and over the next few years, the course grew from 40 hours to 80 hours crammed into four weeks. And my syllabus grew into a small book.

During that first year teaching at the Greg, I met a Jesuit priest who was a renowned literary figure. I told him about my novel *The Canvas of the Soul.* He loved the idea and said he would be happy to read it and offer his feedback. In December of 1995, I received a ten page letter from him, in which he cut my novel to pieces as only a Jesuit could, bluntly telling me how the novel did not work on any level. But, on the bottom of the ninth page he wrote, "However" . . . I turned to page 10 . . . " . . . the writing on St. Francis is the best I have ever read. Throw this book out and write a book about St. Francis."

I followed his advice and tossed out over two years of work and began writing a book about the saint that took over four years to finish.

As I was writing *The Sun and Moon over Assisi,* the hardest thing for me to understand was the saint's love not only for the poor but for poverty itself. It made no sense to me. I had lived such a pampered life, I didn't even know any poor people. St. Francis may have chased after Lady Poverty, but I chased after Brother BMW.

For St. Francis, voluntary poverty was a way for him always to be dependent upon God for everything. I could perhaps understand that on a theoretical level, but on a practical level, it was very difficult to grasp, especially in our culture that promotes personal strength and independence.

In order to better understand, I lived for a month with Franciscan friars serving at St. Francis Inn in Philadelphia. It was another transformational experience. Every conception I had about the homeless and the addicted turned out to be a misconception. I met real people, people just like me in so many ways. It's easy to label a homeless person as lazy or an alcoholic or drug addict as weak. The labels removed my obligation to do anything: it's their fault they are homeless, it's their fault they are addicted. Christ didn't label people or judge people; he reached out to them, he excluded no one.

The people that I blithely dismissed as worthless and those who were dedicating their lives to serving them moved me to want to make a film about the St. Francis Inn. I asked a friend of mine from *Good Morning, America* to help assemble a crew. We made the film in four days. Amazingly, the humble film was broadcast by PBS stations across the country. The film is still shown every Thanksgiving on many PBS stations. Last year the Hallmark Channel aired it.

Over the years, the friars received over $200,000 in donations from people who saw the film and they now have a waiting list of people who want to volunteer. With the money, the Franciscans built a larger soup kitchen to better serve their guests, and added a second floor containing a chapel. Everyday, about sixty poor people, including many recovering addicts, attend the Eucharist at the St. Francis Inn.

That film revealed a new meaning for my life. I knew what I had to do: *put the power of film at the service of the poor.*

Shortly after *The Sun and Moon over Assisi* was published, I met the head of the Order of Friars Minor in Rome. He had read the book and liked it very much. I told him that I was still struggling with the subject of poverty and its meaning for my life. I asked his permission to spend time living with the friars ministering to the poor, so I could create a photo-essay book on the Christian response to poverty.

The Minister General blessed my plan. Within three weeks, I landed in Calcutta, India, and over the course of the next fifteen months I visited thirty-nine cities in eleven nations. All of that travel resulted in a book entitled *When Did I See You Hungry?*

In January of 2002, I formed the San Damiano Foundation. San Damiano was the little church outside the walled city of Assisi where St. Francis heard God ask him to rebuild the Church. We make films that feature individuals and organizations that are helping the poor. They use the films to raise funds. And I show the films at universities and churches in order to raise awareness about the plight of the poor and the need for Christians to do something to relieve this suffering. We seek nothing from those we help. I beg for the funds needed to make the films. Professionals often donate their services. Martin Sheen narrated one film. Bono contributed a song to another. In four years, the San Damiano Foundation has produced seven films. It is emotionally draining and hard work. I make very little money, but I've never been happier or more fulfilled.

Living among the poor in homes that have no electricity or running water is not the hardest part of my job. The hardest part is begging for the funds to produce the films. In an odd way, I learned how to finance my films at the St. Francis Inn. There's a friar there named Brother Xavier. He is a simple man and all the street people love him. One day, he was cooking dinner. A volunteer entered the kitchen and asked, "What are you making, Brother Xavier?"

He answered, "Potato soup."

The volunteer looked around the small, cramped kitchen and didn't see any potatoes. And so he asked, "Where are the potatoes, Brother?"

Brother Xavier answered, "We have no potatoes."

The volunteer asked, "Then how are you making potato soup?"

He said, "The Lord will supply."

Well, you can imagine the volunteer rolling his eyes and thinking, "What a sweet, pious thought, but the people are lining up in the yard and we need to serve them in an hour. A few minutes later, there was a knock at the side door. It was an off-duty Philly cop. He had been at the farmer's market and spotted 50-pound bags of potatoes on sale. He knew he would be passing the Inn and so he bought two bags and threw them in his trunk.

I make my films the way Brother Xavier makes potato soup—by trusting that God will supply what I need.

I've learned a lot about poverty since I walked into that empty church in Rome eleven years ago and my life was changed. Poverty is painful. But far beneath the surface, you find the priceless seed of hope. Not just a fairy-tale hope, but a gritty hope rooted in total dependency upon God. As I walked with the poor, I encountered my own true poverty and the radical truth of the Gospel: only empty hands can hold God.

My encounter with the bloated belly of poverty helped me remove the veil of comfortability from the Gospel and revealed the radical nature of Christianity. Jesus showed us how to love, how to love unconditionally and without limits. And according to Christ, how we love the hungry, the lowly, and the lost, is how we love him; and how we love Christ will be the only litmus test for our entrance into our heavenly home with God for all eternity. And until we enter our eternal home, we are all homeless, even if we live in a palace, because everything on earth is perishable . . . except love.

We are all brothers and sisters, children of the same Creator, and to set ourselves up as higher or better than others is a subtle form of blasphemy. We are all connected, one with all of creation and the Creator. If one amongst us is diminished, we are all diminished.

The Incarnation teaches us that God is humble. The richness of God is revealed in the poverty of Christ. God lives in our poverty and weakness. Jesus embraced and loved the poor and rejected. For Jesus, the poor are sacraments, because they offer a direct way to encounter God. The poor, broken, and rejected are portals through which we can enter fully into the life of Christ. Christ shows us that mercy is more than compassion or justice. Mercy requires us to become one with the poor and hurting, to live their misery as though it were our own. In Christ, we see a God so generous he gives himself away out of love. Christ moved beyond justice to generosity.

We all find God in different ways, but our whole lives are journeys toward God. And on that journey to know God, Jesus makes it abundantly clear that God is to be found in the hungry, the naked, the imprisoned, the homeless, and the downtrodden.

We all know that poverty exists, that there are untold numbers of people living in unimaginably horrible conditions. The growing numbers of homeless in America is on full display in every city. Most people would like to do something to ease the suffering. The sheer number of out-stretched hands begging for our spare change is daunting. But we are busy. Modern life seems hopelessly complex, requiring everyone to become master jugglers, juggling job and family responsibilities. The demands on our time are at once maddening and frustrating. With so many things to do, and so many hands stretching out for help, I think we have developed compassion-fatigue. When we look beyond our borders, to the dire poverty around the world we are overwhelmed by the need. War, famine, brutal dictatorships, natural disasters, economic recessions, and corrupt governments have created a huge exodus of refugees living in a squalor that defies description. We grow weary from stories on television and in newspapers documenting the plight of the poor in places such as Darfur, Kenya, and Haiti, to name only a handful of countries that easily spring to mind. The cumulative effect of all the tragic stories leaves us feeling helpless to do anything about it. So, we turn away and keep busy.

But the Gospel tells us we cannot turn away, cannot divert our eyes and hearts from the suffering caused by chronic poverty. My hope is that the films produced by the San Damiano Foundation will connect the viewer emotionally to the poor. The films look at the problem of domestic and global poverty through the lens of spirituality. We need a new way to look at the poor and a new way to respond to the poor. We need to look through eyes of faith, no matter what faith we follow; and we need to respond with a heart of faith. And it will not be easy. It will take time. Meditating on the plight of the poor, our role in their plight, and the spiritual response to the plight is vital.

While spending time among the poor, I've learned the importance of relationships and how interdependent we are on each other. For St. Francis of Assisi prayers were not an escape from the world but an entrance into it. As St. Francis grew in relationship with God during prolonged periods of solitude and prayer his growing awareness of God's presence within himself gave him a new way to look at the world around him and helped him see God's presence within others. Because he had been touched and embraced by God's diffusive and self-giving love Francis himself had no choice but to become more loving toward everyone he encountered. The growing awareness of God's presence within all creation and especially within all humanity reached its apex when the saint embraced and kissed a leper. For Francis, the Incarnation gave birth to compassion which enabled him to see in the rotting flesh of a leper the self-giving love of God.

I've learned to see the poor and the marginalized, the alcoholic and the drug addict, the mentally ill and the homeless not as objects of pity and charity but as brothers and sisters with whom I'm intimately related. The longer I walk with the poor—and with Jesus—the more I see the need to put to death the idea of my own self-sufficiency. To think of myself as separate from God and all of creation, including the poor, is an illusion.

As I traveled, I began to see more clearly how turning my back on the poor was turning my back on Jesus. My exposure to those saddled with extreme poverty uncovered my own clinging selfishness. I came to see how consuming more than I needed was stealing from those in need. Perhaps St. Francis understood that it would be hard for him to feel true compassion for the poor and the weak as long he sought comfort and required security for himself. I think St. Francis understood that compassion was far removed from pity and sympathy, that compassion grew out of an awareness of our common humanity. For St. Francis service to the poor was not optional. It was a requirement for the follower of Christ.

While we busy ourselves striving for power and control, the Gospel proclaims a different approach: live a life of utter dependence on and receptivity to God. Accepting that spiritual reality makes spiritual growth and fulfillment possible. The Gospel invites us to live with contradiction—when one has nothing, one has everything.

If the Gospel is not about love and justice, it has been reduced to mere sentimentality. Jesus denounced power that leads to injustice and poverty; he asked us to share what we have with others. Christianity does not turn away from the cross and suffering; it enters it. Of course, we don't like hearing that.

In modern-day, consumer-driven America, we continually feel the need for the accumulation of goods and security. We have ignored what God has put in our hearts to do: love one another. Instead we are being consumed by consuming, reaching the point where there is no way out. We have deceived ourselves into thinking we can follow Christ without becoming one with the poor, that we can know and love God without loving others, and not just friends and family and those that love us back! Jesus says that's easy, even pagans do that. Christ calls us to a different, deeper kind of love: a love for the unlovable, for those who cannot give back, even for our enemies. Christ said that at the end of our lives that is the litmus test we all will face.

Jesus identified with the poor and the rejected, showing us that God lies waiting where the world never thinks to look. And Saint Francis reminds me to look at my relationship to everything in my life. He makes me take a second look at what "ownership" means. He tells me that everything belongs to God, who in His infinite love allows me to use them. This prevents me from clutching to things as "mine," and instead fills me with gratitude for the generosity of God who has lent me all I need. That shift in consciousness lifts a tremendous burden from my heart. Rather than holding on to what I own, I enjoy what has been temporarily lent to me. Everything is gift; everything is God's. Francis teaches me that I'm merely a humble steward gently holding things in trust, enjoying God's bounty without becoming attached to anything.

Poverty of spirit does not refer to an economic condition. It reflects the human reality that we are poor before God and, consequently, we need to depend radically on God alone for true fulfillment. We must be on guard not to confuse the necessities of life with luxuries. The humble simplicity that embodies poverty of spirit stands in stark contrast with the unbridled pursuit of comfort, power, pleasure, and riches which permeates a society that prizes possession as a good in itself. Poverty of spirit is a means of maintaining a continual attitude of dying to self without succumbing to self-hatred or causing a lack of self-esteem. We need to die to self because it is the only way to be fully alive to God.

Christ-like transformation is not concerned with acquiring more but in letting go of more, and becoming more present to those with less. The best way you can show your love of God is to be merciful to others. Every act of mercy and kindness brings us closer to the reality of God. Growing closer to God is our real job in life. We need to open our eyes and see the many blessings God has given us and then we must share them freely with others. Do not be afraid of enjoying the full freedom of giving your life away. In *Seeds of Contemplation*, Thomas Merton reminds us: "We do not detach ourselves from things in order to attach ourselves to God, but rather we become detached from ourselves in order to see and use all things in and for God."

## *A Prefatory Word from St. Bonaventure*

In the fall of 1259, St Bonaventure, the great Franciscan saint, was longing to satisfy the deep desire of his spirit for peace. He retreated to a hermitage at Mount LaVerna in Tuscany in order to drink in the silence and solitude. While there, St. Bonaventure composed his masterpiece, *The Journey of the Human Person into God,* which is more commonly known as *The Soul's Journey into God.* At the end of the Prologue, he wrote the following caveat to his readers:

*I ask, therefore,*
*that you give more attention*
*to the intent of the writer*
*than to the work itself,*
*more to the things said*
*than to the uncultivated language,*
*more to the truth than to the attractiveness,*
*more to the stimulation of affect*
*than to intellectual enrichment.*
*So that this might happen,*
*it is important that you*
*not run through these reflections*
*in a hurry,*
*but that you take your time*
*and ruminate over them slowly.*

While not daring to compare this humble book with that of the great saint, I do think it would be best to heed his advice and go slowly through these pages also.

# Thoughts of a blind beggar

# PART ONE

## The Praises to Be Said at All Hours

Holy, holy, holy Lord God Almighty,
Who is, and Who was, and Who is to come.
> And let us praise and glorify Him forever.
O Lord our God, You are worthy to receive
praise, glory and honor and blessing.
> And let us praise and glorify Him forever. . . .
Bless the Lord, all you works of the Lord.
> And let us praise and glorify Him forever.
Sing praise to our God, all you His servants
and you who fear God, the small and the great.
> And let us praise and glorify Him forever.
Let heaven and earth praise Him Who is glorious.
> And let us praise and glorify Him forever.
Every creature in heaven, on earth and under the earth;
and in the sea and those which are in it.
> And let us praise and glorify Him forever.
Glory to the Father and to the Son and to the Holy Spirit.
> And let us praise and glorify Him forever.
As it was in the beginning, is now, and will be forever.
> And let us praise and glorify Him forever.

All powerful, most holy, most high God: all good, supreme good, totally good. You Who alone are good, may we give You all praise, all glory, all thanks, all honor, all blessing, and all good. So be it! So be it! *Amen.*

Saint Francis of Assisi
—*Early Documents*, Volume I, page 161

# The Messiness of Life

*We live in a world that is filled with pain. The planet is covered with people who are overwhelmed by suffering. Wars, monstrous acts of terrorism, famine, economic injustice, chronic poverty, drug addiction, disease and natural disasters are killing people every day. We are impotent when it comes to making the pain go away. Life is hard and messy and painful. Hurt abounds and hope is in short supply. Jesus did not clean up every mess or relieve all the pain He encountered. He simply told us to take the pain and the mess of our lives and place them before God. Even then, the answers to the riddles of our lives are not always perceivable or even obtainable. Jesus teaches us to live with the questions, to live with the pain. Peace, He suggests, is found in faith. God is bigger than we are; and we, in our weakness, need to lean on the strong arm of God. Cures and answers may not come to light, but faith, hope, and love change who we are and how we deal with the messiness and pain of life.*

### The Blind Beggar

Be like the blind beggar at Jericho,
seated at the side of the road,
and stretch out open hands
to the silence of God.

Humility is the heart of Christianity,
and the gateway to prayer.

Without prayer, God dies in our hearts.

Prayer is being present.

### Cup of Coffee

Each day needs to be a pilgrimage
into my own heart.

"This day is yours, Lord,"
I say each day upon rising.
Yet, before I even finish
my first cup of coffee,
the day has become mine.

God never shouts to be heard over our noise.
Only silence gives God a chance to speak.

The soul that waits on God,
patiently and unhurriedly,
will eventually be filled
with the realization he or she
is infinitely loved.

### First Step

I need to stand before God
in a stance of constant conversion.

The acknowledgment of our own weakness
is the first step toward an acknowledgment
of Christ's strength.

In condemning others,
I am avoiding the more difficult task
of knowing myself.

### Still Life

Contemplation requires
tranquility and patience.

The art of contemplating divine truths
grows out of the art of remaining still.

To be a contemplative is
to be receptive to the divine Word.

### Standing in Line

Even in a crowd I stand alone before God.

Solitude can be found while standing
in line at a supermarket or bank.

Within each of us, without exception,
there is a longing to pass beyond finite things.

Kindness is essential to restore
our interior Garden of Eden.

### Kiss the Joy

Desires rob us of freedom.

Dependence on reason is unreasonable.

Don't try to possess the object of your delight . . .
kiss the joy as it flies.

Sanctify the present moment.

### God Knows

Only God understands God.

Even when your plans do not work out,
God's plan does.

The sacred dwells in the secular.

### Undivided

A pure heart is an undivided heart.

Only the pure of heart
see God in everything.

The glorious presence of God
radiates through all creation.

In the garden of the human spirit
there is a tiny blade of understanding
urging us to look hard at everything
and seek God in all that we see.

### Knock, Knock

Physical solitude is nothing
without an inner solitude.

Seek God in the ordinary events of daily life.

No moment is insignificant.
Incarnation may break through at any time.

Seek, knock, ask, plead.

### Radiant Love

God speaks to us even in the smallest
and most ordinary events of daily life.

God's love does not shout, it whispers.

Be still and hear God whisper
soft words of fondest love.

Listen . . . don't think.

Love should radiate, not dominate.

### Not Fickle

My awareness of God's mysterious presence
within me
helps me become more aware
of the same presence within others.

To love others as Jesus loves them
is an extremely difficult,
if not impossible,
task, yet it must be
our primary goal as Christians.

The key to attaining happiness
is to give it away.
But we love hanging onto
what we've got.

Divine love is not fickle.
It has only one desire:
total self-giving.

Happiness grows only in the garden
of unconditional love.

Charity is the art of knowing
how to do the will of God.


## Mine

Self-indulgence leads to spiritual dryness.

Desires give birth to desires.

Consume less.

Everything belongs to God.
Nothing belongs to us.

Enjoy without owning.

God alone calms and satisfies all our desire.


## First Fruit

I am not my own horizon.
Jesus is always leading me
to travel beyond myself
to the Father.

Humility is the first fruit
of honesty with oneself.
True humility plunges one
into adoration of God.

Humility takes training.

Humility increases with self-knowledge.

### Life and Death

Cling to yourself
and you will lose yourself.

Communion with God is life;
separation from God is death.

Walk humbly behind Christ.

Humility, detachment, charity and compassion
are the cornerstones of the Christian life.

### Little Ol' Me

Emptiness is the one true reality
we all are desperate to bury.

My poverty is a cry to God.

Humility is an expression of the reality
of our littleness and powerlessness.

## *Forgetting God*

Whenever I feel a sense of self-assurance
and self-importance
I am in danger of forgetting God.

Pride prevents us from accepting God's help.

Avarice is defeated by compassion for the poor.


## *A Ticket to Heaven?*

God reveals my sinfulness to me,
not to make me feel guilty
but to offer me forgiveness
and freedom from the bondage
of destructive behavior.

Penance paves the way for continual conversion.

Redemption isn't a ticket to heaven . . .
it simply means a soul has been redeemed
—set free—
from self-interest.


## *No Guts, No Glory*

When it comes to following Christ
without reservation,
I know exactly what to do.
What I lack is the courage to do it.

Surrender is never easy.
When Jesus was called to his final surrender,
he sweated blood.

Virtue is attained only by hard work.
We must struggle to grow in love,

prayer, self-control, and compassion,
which are the roots of all virtue.

## Heart and Soul

Transformation is not possible where we,
not God,
are secretly in control,
cavalierly pretending we "know-it-all."

By recognizing my weakness
I become strong.

God is humble.
God lives in
our poverty and weakness.

Simplicity safeguards the spirit
from distractions and leads it to God.

Love and trust are
the heart and soul of simplicity.

## Uncovered

You can't be converted
without becoming naked
and seeing clearly
all your faults and weaknesses.

Passion is an expression of
love or hunger.

Do not judge others;
instead, live with God.

The closer you come to God
the more compassion you will have
for your neighbor.

## Making Headway

Stop measuring your progress.
In fact, let go of the idea of "progress."

Look for "moments" of prayer.

Prayer helps us remember
that our life is a journey
to God.

Growth in purity is linked
to increasing our ability
to establish and maintain
solitude of soul for God alone.

## Conflict Resolution

Prayer is hanging on to God,
stubbornly clinging to God.

Beg for the grace of prayer.

The universal lack of an interior life
is a key element behind the rash
of violent political and religious conflicts
that plague so many nations.

## Entering the Darkness

When I pray using my mind,
I find I have nothing to say.
Prayer is a gift of the Spirit.

The more I pray,
the deeper I enter into the darkness
of the absence of evidence.

### *You Are What You Eat*

Prayer is about loving
and being loved.

Simplicity is in harmony with contemplation.

Prayer deepens with purification of faults.

You grow into what you dwell upon.

Progress along the spiritual path
is fueled by desire.

### *The Bottom Line*

Prayer stimulates a mindfulness of God,
which in turn stimulates acts of love and mercy.

Love is service.
It is the emptying of self.
It is losing in order to find.

Acknowledging my own weakness
increases my ability
to be more merciful toward others.

The Christian life can be reduced to this:
live the beatitudes.

### *Ready for God*

The more you pray,
the more you will become
poor, plain and empty.
And ready for God.

Prayer consists of becoming aware.

We experience God's love
in proportion to our experience
of our own weakness.

In the shadows of our own weakness,
God extends a loving hand of help.

### *Shut Up*

If Christ is the center of my life,
then I am not.
This is good.

Tell your ego to shut up.

Let yourself be loved;
let yourself be acted upon by God.

Contentment is the daughter of simplification.

Faith in Christ means I allow my life
to be illuminated and sustained by His life.

### *Letting Go*

Poverty is another word for "letting go."

Detachment makes one powerful.

To keep silence is to keep listening.

### *The Surest Way*

The longer I walk with the poor
—and with Jesus—
the more I see the need to put to death
the idea of my own self-sufficiency.

To think of myself as separate
from God and all of creation
is an illusion.

To be in communion with those who are suffering
is the surest way to chip away
at the notion you are a separate self,
detached from the rest of creation.

Letting go of my life
is the surest way
to a life of abundance.

Eternal life is not something that happens
in the future;
it is now.

## *Nothing Easy*

In solitude, seek God,
not consolation or ecstasy.

Spiritual life involves struggle and effort.
Anyone who wants to love
distrusts whatever is easy.

I was becoming smug about my spiritual progress
when I was knocked off my high horse
by this thought:
I still harbor aspirations beyond Christ.

Incarnate the Gospel
before you proclaim it.

## *Drum Beat*

The loud drum beat of fear and anxiety
can be quieted by contemplation.

When Christ reveals his heart to us,
He also reveals our sinfulness.

The most deadly characteristic of sin
is its ease of repetition.

God does not seek perfection in us;
God wants repentance.

Jesus does not promise happiness.
He proclaims the beatitudes.

## *A Change of Mind*

The spiritual life is won or lost
between the ears.
Our minds must be transformed
by Christ.
We need to change the way we think . . .
we need mind renewal!
We need to put on the mind
of Christ.

In the letter to the Romans, Paul writes,
"Whatever does not proceed from faith is sin."
Wow.
That is very radical and extremely tough.
But Paul understands that anything
that cuts against our faith
destroys the unity and fullness of life
created by God and that is God.
Does everything I do proceed from faith?
I think not.
This is trouble.

My faith must move beyond the realm
of my private life.

## *The Impossibility of the Cross*

The Cross is a sign of eternal charity.

God's ways are so profoundly different from ours
that it is impossible to understand them.

At the foot of the Cross,
humility, poverty, and despair
are sanctified.

19

### Doing the Impossible

Doing God's will requires
we bring our mind, heart and will
into harmony with our faith.

The measure of our love of our enemies
is the only reliable indicator
of our spiritual progress.

Jesus is crucified again in the flesh of
thousands of innocent Iraqis suffering
from the effects of violence
perpetrated by a "Christian" nation
that chooses not to be a witness
to God's reconciling love.
The Gospel is radical and demanding.
And impossible . . . until you accept the fact
that you can't live it without Christ's help.

### A Homeless Man

Faith requires we surrender
our wills.

I live in an overcrowded house
of false values.

A homeless, naked, dying man on the cross asks:
are you reasonably comfortable?

Calvary is less about the extreme suffering
endured by Christ on the cross
and more about
the extreme love
that drew Him to the cross.

At the foot of the Cross
words sink into silence
as I look up and ask,
for the love of God,
if I am ready
to follow Christ.

## Doing What You Love

Salvation is discovering
who you really are.

The surest way to death
is not to discover
what you love.

Knowing what you love
helps you reorder your life
in order to do what you love.
When you are doing what you love,
you become love.

## Not Optional

Test your love for God;
love wants more than anything else
to be in the presence of the beloved.

Adoration is not optional.

Be governed by eternity, not time.

There is no time—there is only
the ever-present now.

## *A Pure Heart*

Our hearts are as great as our love.

I must empty my heart of all selfishness,
before God can fill it with love.

It is easier to be self-centered
than to be patient and loving.

We can only love truly
when our hearts are free
of the self-centered desires
of pride, ambition, and lust.

A true act of love is one
that expects nothing in return.

The more aware we become
of the Divine Presence within us,
the more we shall forget ourselves
and become more serene and pure of heart.

## *Love Is the Key*

Jesus asks us to love as God loves—
without counting the cost
or holding anything back.
Love gives all away.
Love frees us to act for the good of another
rather than for ourselves.
God's love is unbiased and all-embracing.
It does not ask who we are
or how successful we are at what we do.

Being an instrument of peace requires us
to embrace the enemy in pardon.

To give freely what we have freely received
—namely, God's love—
is the purest form of evangelization.
Following the example of Christ
will lead us to go poor among the poor,
without power, without purse, without provisions,
with charity and respect for those we encounter.
We must seek peace above all else
and then do good at every opportunity.
If our efforts at sharing God's love
are warmly received, fine;
if not, we should move on.
Our lives are our sermons,
and our preaching should be benign and gentle,
spoken with meekness and humility.

### *Hail Mary*

Mary gave God a human heart.
She gives me Christ's heart.

Mary is a model for meekness.
Meekness is truly a divine disposition.

Hail Mary, full of grace,
help me to pray.

O most pure Theotokos,
teach me childlike
humility of heart
and purity of spirit.

## *Planting a Seed*

God is near.
God is warm.
God is tender.
It is time we stress these softer
attributes of God.

Plant a seed of gratefulness in your heart,
so that day by day
you grow more thankful to God
for the overflowing goodness and mercy
God has lavished upon you.

Only when I am able to see my own unholiness
can I begin to see the sacredness of all creation.

## *Listen to the Silence*

Silence allows us to live within,
helps us to concentrate on the serious,
profound inner mysteries of life.
Noise takes us out of ourselves,
and distracts and scatters our thoughts.

Silence is not simply a wordless state;
it is an attentive waiting.
Deep, spiritually-active silence
allows us to hear the unity of life.

## A Gift of Grace

All opposites are united in Christ.
With Christ, there is richness in poverty,
fullness in hunger
and joy in sorrow.

We are all vulnerable and incomplete—
and in need of God's love, grace, and mercy.

All good things are
a gift of grace.

The soul loves simplicity and chastity.

Without purity, we can not "see" God.

Grace is the breath of Love.

## Pilgrim's Progress

The quest for God is a journey,
a pilgrimage to the depths of the soul.

The quest requires a listening heart,
an ear quickened to the silent voice of God,
and vigilant spirit actively waiting and watching.

To be a pilgrim is to live on life's threshold,
walking on the edge of reality,
striving for what lies beyond the reality
we see with our flawed human eyes.

### *Make Believe Time*

God is present and living in the world.
Better to see the Lord here on earth
then to try to penetrate the mysteries
of another world beyond death.

Stop brooding over the incomprehensible
which is beyond the power of understanding.

Punctuate your day with thoughts of God,
recalling God's unselfish,
self-giving love for us.

Recapture your childhood faculty
for make-believe.
Let go of your sophisticated ways.

Stand before God
in a stance of conversion.

### *Day by Day*

Holiness seems beyond our grasp,
so we settle for mediocrity.

Transformation is a daily event.

The main thrust of one's energy
must be applied to
spiritual growth.

Pray always.

Cling to Jesus.

# PART TWO

# Lauds

## *The Prayer before the Crucifix*

Most High,
glorious God,
enlighten the darkness of my heart
and give me
true faith,
certain hope,
and perfect charity,
sense and knowledge,
Lord,
that I may carry out
Your holy and true command.

Saint Francis of Assisi
—*Early Documents*, Volume I, page 40

# Walking toward the Light

*I am a sinner not immune from temptation. Often I stumble, often I succumb to the deception of my ego. My heart is fickle, my faith weak. Holiness seems beyond my reach. Yet, each day, I pick myself up and keep walking toward the Light, toward the day when I have finally emptied myself of all that is not God. Unity with God does not happen in a flash; it is not won by a lottery ticket, instantly bestowing the riches of heaven upon you. Unity with God takes time, as day by day, month by month, year by year we slowly and deliberately let go of more stuff cluttering our tiny hearts in order to make room for the infinite source of love and life.*

## *Good Morning*

Each day I must open myself up
to the splendor of God.

If you greet sunrise with God in your heart
and a prayer on your lips,
your day stands a better chance
of reflecting God's love, mercy, and justice,
and you will be better able
to treat others the way God would.

When you give God your heart,
He gives you His eyes,
so you may begin to see things
the way He sees them—
through eyes of love,
mercy, and compassion.

Compassion helps us
from clinging to ourselves;
it helps us see our kinship
with all living beings.

Today, did you add to the world's harmony?

## *Another Day, the Same Question*

Everyday, God asks the same question:
Are you willing?

Let God lead.

God loves mercy and tenderness,
Yet we all too often,
in countless ways small and large,
turn from these godly virtues.

## Handle with Care

Every moment is a moment of grace—
if my eyes and heart are open.

Handle all life,
and every moment of your life,
with care, respect, and love.

Morning prayer is the most important prayer
of the day . . .
it sets the tone for all that will follow.

## A Sacred Space

We can turn any space into a sacred space.
A bedroom corner can be a basilica,
a portal into the mystery and meaning of life.

Waiting, waiting, waiting.
Our spiritual lives are a vigil
of waiting.
We wait with hope
for the advent of God.

Yet as we wait for God,
God is already here with us.
And we are with God,
yet not fully so,
and so we wait,
living with paradox and expectancy.

Spiritual transformation
never ends . . . it is always new,
forever beginning.

## *The Everyday Stuff of Life*

We all love big, flashy miracles,
but when you see the wonder,
the miracle within,
all of life becomes miraculous,
and the everyday stuff of life—
the ordinary and mundane tasks of living—
are transformed into moments
of beauty and joy.

The gift of self-abandonment allows us
to live fully in the present moment.

We are the measure of our possibilities and limitations.
God has no restrictions or limitations.

## *Hidden in the Ordinary*

Listen to the silence of nature
and you will hear a symphony
singing the praises of God.

In the incubator of silence,
wisdom and tolerance are born.

Leave room for the unexpected,
the moment of insight.
Don't shut the door on tiny epiphanies.

Every day carries the experience of presence
and absence.

Prayer helps you see the extraordinary
hidden in the ordinary.

Our prayer life needs to move from being
mechanical and extrinsic
to being mystical and intrinsic.

The only thing standing between me and God
is me.

My sins expose my fallibility . . . and
my complete dependence upon God alone.

## The Streets of Life

The spiritual life does not lift us
above the human condition —
its misery, problems, confrontations,
pain, and difficulties.
Spiritual life plunges us deeply
into our humanity.
It would be nice
to sit in church all day,
hands clasped in prayer,
drinking the ecstasy of the Lord.
But that is unrealistic;
we must enter into the marketplace,
walk the alleys of commerce.
We must help each other
out of the ditches into which we fall.
In the streets of life
we encounter God.
Everything human is divine.

## A Singing Cloud

All of creation sings of the splendor of God.
Today I heard a cloud sing
as the rays of the sun cut through it.

Along the spiritual path,
the concept of reward and punishment
must evolve (or dissolve) into
the concept of wholeness and division.

Comparison involves thinking about yourself,
which is dangerous
because it ends in our conferring
undue importance upon ourselves.

## Finding Jesus

Finding Jesus in new and unexpected places
is the essence of the Christian life.

The blending of the inspirational
and the incarnational
creates a holistic spirituality.

Prayer, work, and play: the trinity of a
balanced, healthy, and rewarding life.

## Transfigured by Grace

Christ is radically present
in the entire universe
as its ultimate fulfillment.

In creation we contemplate
a manifestation of God's face,
of God's presence—
and our souls are set afire
with charity
for all of creation,
leading us to embrace
the whole world,
a world deformed by sin,
yet transfigured by grace.

## A Humble Disguise

Through creation we can pick up
the footprint of God.

Beauty is a vestige of God.
God made the flower
and your reaction to it
picks up a vestige of God.

Oh how we long to find God
in some moment of spiritual ecstasy,
looking for the Divine in some spectacular
or extraordinary event.
Yet God comes to us,
if we are to believe
—fully believe—
what scripture says,
in a humble disguise,
in unexpected places.
God comes to us
poor, hungry, thirsty,
diseased, imprisoned, alone, and lonely.
God comes to us in a homeless old woman
forced to use a public street for a toilet.
God comes to us in people, places, and ways
that make it difficult for us to see Him
or receive Him.
We don't find God
where we expect or want to find Him.

I saw Jesus over and over again
in a leprosarium in Manaus, Brazil.

## *God's Healing Hands*

The real sin hidden within the plague of
global poverty
where millions upon millions are suffering
from hunger and curable disease
is our inexplicable indifference,
our complicity and complacency.
The Gospel tells us we must not look away
from the suffering, must not ignore the poor.
The Gospel tells us to embrace
the suffering and the weak,
to be God's healing hands.

According to Jesus,
you cannot honor God
and dishonor the poor at the same time,
nor can you wage war
and worship God at the same time.

Watch how a person treats
the poor and the hungry,
the sick and the stranger,
and you will know that person's view of life.

You can measure the value of spiritual experiences
by the extent to which
they return the individual to the physical world
with an enhanced sense
of responsibility toward others.

## Stop Running

We do not need to run and catch God;
we need to stop running
and be caught by God.

The One who has always been
is always present.
We are the ones too busy
to be present to God's presence.

On the road to God,
words eventually dissolve into silence.

God loves to surprise us.

## Our Gateway to God

Perhaps the single biggest need
busy people face today is quiet.
It is impossible to touch God
on a deep level if we do not recover
the essential gift and grace of quiet and silence
that make us aware of God's holy presence.
Far more than the absence of noise,
silence is an opportunity,
our gateway to God.

The best way to approach God is
to proceed in humility, simplicity, and poverty,
and to enter into the silence of God's presence,
and then patiently sit in prayer
and wait until God elects to speak.

In silence, we are able to meet
our deepest self.
When we have found
our authentic self,

we are free
to give ourselves away,
to give ourselves back to God.

Contemplation without action
is merely conceptualization.
Likewise, action without contemplation
is merely busyness.


## A Crowded Bus in Rome

Wherever you are,
whatever you are doing,
God is there.
Strive to feel God's presence and warmth
in the ordinary moments of the day.
The commonplace is also a divine place.

The sacred is not here or there but everywhere.

God is on a crowded bus in Rome.
The challenge is to become aware of it.

God is rarely where I think God should be.

God is in the quiet whispers of the trees
and in the noisy rattlings
of a New York City subway train.


## A Weather-Beaten Old Barn

An incredibly beautiful world
lies silently all around us all of the time,
and it remains unseen, a lost paradise,
until some quiet miracle opens our eyes

and we see everything afresh.
By grace, seeing deeply into a flower
or a weather-beaten old barn
or even the tormented face of a homeless person,
we catch a glimpse of Paradise,
a vestige of God.

As the opposite of pride,
humility reflects honesty, a holistic sense of reality,
and a keen awareness
of the awesomeness of the universe
and the profound mystery of God.
Growth in humility is a sign
of maturing holiness.

## Homecoming

Let go of certainty.
Embrace the Mystery.

God is a homecoming celebration.

Christ's resurrection still happens to us.

## Hiding in the Shadows

My wealth lies in God's love for me;
my poverty lies in my lack of love for God.

The hunger for God can never be satisfied.
The more we taste of God,
the more intense our hunger becomes.
The journey to God is eternal.
The more we experience,
the more there is to experience.
God is inexhaustible,
and far beyond our capacity to apprehend.

Recognizing God in a burning bush would be easy;
seeing God in the shadows is very hard.
For the most part, God hides in the shadows,
and rarely appears in a burning bush.
We banish the shadows
with the bright lights
of empty diversions.

## Who's There?

God was knocking on the door
of my soul for 47 years.
One day, I heard it.
God's patience was greater
than my deafness.

## A Still Lake

The more aware I become of
the perfection of Christ,
the better I am able to see
my own imperfections.

Being able to look beyond imperfections
—your own and others—
is the key to being happy.

The merciful see the best in everything.

A pure heart is like a still lake
which reflects the majesty of God.

## *Empty Hands*

The world demands more and more from us.
God only asks for empty hands.

I missed yesterday.
I was too busy to see it.

God resides in the beyond
that lies within.

We find it more comfortable to put limits on God,
and in doing so we create
a spiritual poverty within us.

Allow God to turn your life
upside-down and inside-out.
Allow God to topple your expectations.
Journey beyond comfort.
Pursue true knowledge.

## *Just One Question*

I have only one question to answer:
Is God's presence within me
merely "a" reality
or
is it "the" reality?

## *Vision Correction*

Authentic gratitude embraces all of life.

Solitude allows the soul to look
upon the pieces and see the unity.

Poverty helps me see beauty
in an earthenware pot.

## *Mask of Humility*

Do I hide my pride
behind a mask of humility?

As we grow in self-knowledge,
we grow in true humility.

Humility frees us from the tyranny
of the ego's power.

When an understanding of who we are
and where we came from
permeates our entire being
we are truly on the road to redemption.

Seeing my own emptiness and impermanence
prompted me to fall to my knees and pray.

Once the clouds of self-deception
have been blown away by prayer,
the need for repentance becomes clear:
we are not who, or how,
we once thought we were.

## *Forgetting God*

Self-absorption makes me forget the reality of God.
Humility frees me from absorption in myself.

Hope is the fruit of charity.

To be human is to be poor.

Don't allow luxuries
to become necessities.

### Center Stage

All life is a cry to God.

Happy are those who know
the need for God.

Give your incapacity to God.

If God is not center stage
then you are in the wrong play.

### Self Service

Self-will causes us to act on our fears.

Self-conceit and pride are road blocks
to the reception of grace.

Self-restraint is essential
to living a life for and with God.

### Heaven and Hell

Spiritual transformation requires turning
selfish desire into selfless desire.

Your ego must choose between
heaven and hell.

Flee illusion. Search for God.

Oh how we hesitate to give ourselves fully
to the search.

## *My Only Joy*

I would never deliberately choose self over God—
except that I do so
in countless little ways
every day without realizing it.

Is God my only joy?
If not, I have not fully surrendered.

Who we are can only be revealed
by the love and mercy of God.

When you are free enough to be nothing,
God can use you for anything.


## *A Light in the Darkness*

My anguish, my fear, my temptations
can become a path to God
if I acknowledge my littleness and my weakness
and transform them into a trust
that God alone can bring
light into my darkness,
if I abandon myself completely
and take refuge in God's love.

When we embark on an inward journey
we eventually arrive at a place
of keen awareness of our own
powerlessness and hopelessness,
and, like Christ,
must yield to the mercy of God.

### *Poverty Road*

At the moment when Christ said,
"Not my will, but Yours be done,"
He experienced the true crucifixion
and became a living sacrifice.
We need to experience a crucifixion
every day . . . to nail our wills to the cross
and surrender our wills to the will of God.
Are we living sacrifices?

Christ became poor and emptied himself
of everything . . . for us.

I go to God with my hands full . . .
and ask for more.
St. Francis of Assisi was willing to go to God
with empty hands.
For him, the only thing that mattered
was utter trust in God,
and the saint's adult life
was a continual witness
to the realization that total trust
cannot exist until we have lost all self-trust
and are rooted in poverty.

My efforts at approaching perfect trust
are woefully feeble.
St. Francis said the road to God
is straight and narrow:
the road is poverty.
We must be willing to go to God
with empty hands,
trusting God for everything.

A life of prayer and poverty
helped St. Francis of Assisi
unearth an essential spiritual truth:

Total trust in God cannot exist
until we have lost all self-trust.

The most difficult of fasts does not involve
abstinence from food.
Far more difficult is to fast
from your own selfishness.
I once managed to stay on such a fast
for 2½ hours
and it was hell.

## Rules and Regulations

To renounce sin means to work at defeating
our natural weaknesses and selfish passions.
To sin is to refuse God's love.

God is not interested in rules and regulations;
God is interested in love and communion.

To be human is to make mistakes.
To be human is to be in constant
need of forgiveness.
God knows this.

## Heart to Heart

Prayer creates a listening heart.

God demands a lot of time.
In prayer, quantity produces quality.

Sit with Jesus
and allow His heart
to speak to your heart.

### The Emptiness of the Desert

Prayer helps us transcend
our preoccupation with the self,
and teaches us how to embrace the other.

Grace prompts us to pray,
and praying opens us up to even more grace.

Jesus often sought the emptiness of the desert
to experience a fuller union with God.

### A Trap

A humble prayer offered
with trust and perseverance
is always answered.

Stop trying to be relevant.
It is a trap.
Only God is relevant.

God is far beyond us and deep within us.

### Salvation

Prayer should not turn into a self-analytical couch.

Salvation: God loves me and I love God.

Our biggest challenge: restore harmony within ourselves.

St. Augustine said that a friend is someone
who knows all about us
and loves us anyway.
That is a perfect description of God.

### My Only Hope

At its essence, prayer is not about
asking for divine favors.
The primary purpose of prayer
is to assist us in continual
abandonment to God.

Christianity is not meant to be a comfort:
it is a Cross, carried daily.

Christ is Risen is my only hope.

### Soulmates

Praying creates an awareness of God's presence
in the here-and-now,
and that awareness elicits a response.

Prayer and charity are soulmates.

A life of contemplation and a life of action
are not mutually exclusive.

### No Words

Deep silence is profoundly liberating.

Prayerful silence is more than a lack of words;
it is a state of alert stillness.
The point is not to rest,
but to concentrate and focus
the heart and mind on God.
Beneath the appearance of passivity
is an active state of attentiveness.

In deep silence, we are fully awake,
fully open and one with God.

To enter the silence of meditation
is to enter our own poverty
as we renounce words and images,
as we renounce thoughts and imagination,
as we renounce our concepts and intellect
and we sit alert,
waiting to hear from God . . .
even if we must wait a lifetime.

Washing the dishes can be an act of prayer.


## Lost

Without solitude and silence,
I easily lose my self. And God.

Solitude is a presence, not an absence.

Silence is the soul of simplicity.

Simplicity is the sister of purity.


## Doomed

The frenzied pace of life today
easily leaves you feeling
disorientated and unbalanced.
The crush of time and competition
has nearly squeezed contemplation
out of existence.
Without regular periods of
stillness and contemplation,
we are doomed.

As we enter the age of globalization,
human survival may very well
hinge on the ability of
the world's religions
to enter into a spirit of
genuine dialogue.

We all have a vocation
to contemplation.
Genuine contemplation flows
naturally into action.


## An Inner Voice

Silence is an expression of love and strength.

Solitude gives you the ability to hear
an inner voice longing to tell you
the truth about yourself.

If you don't listen, you will never learn.

If we are constantly talking,
God will be unable to teach you anything.


## A Time for Stillness

We must guard against the onslaught
of distractions our culture hurls at us each day.
We need to incorporate structured time
for spiritual reading and reflection.

We need to create time for stillness,
for dwelling in nothingness,

carving places in our daily schedules
for contemplation, meditation, or prayer.

We need to be less concerned with
doing so many things,
and instead develop our innate capacity
for simply being—
being fully present to the integrity and capacity of
each moment.

More often than not,
I seem to be far from God.
But in those moments,
frequent as they are,
God is near.
So near, I do not have to struggle
to find God,
for God is already seeking me,
rushing to embrace me.
But it is only in stillness
that I can sense God's movement,
God's presence.

Whether we are aware of it or not,
God's love is continually coursing
through our very veins.

Meditative walks and listening to sacred music
are excellent ways to help cultivate
inner stillness and silence.

Prayer cleanses your heart
and separates you
from the transitory allurements
of the world.

## The Interior Abyss

Entering into solitude with the idea
of affirming ourselves,
separating oneself from others,
even interiorly,
in order to be different,
or by intensifying one's individual self-awareness
is not in harmony with
the purity required for spiritual growth.

For the Christian, pure solitude is a place
of self-emptying
in order to experience union with Christ;
in the interior abyss we become detached
from our petty false self
and open ourselves up
to the vastness of the Infinite.

## Perishable Things

It is in stillness that we find our emptiness,
the emptiness that can only be filled
by welcoming God into our hearts.

Do not be seduced
by perishable things.

Detachment reflects the realization
that God alone matters.

To pray is to surrender your own power.
When you enter into prayer
you must leave your self behind.

## *Giving Everything*

Christ shows us that mercy
is more than compassion or justice.
Mercy requires us to become one
with the poor and hurting,
to live their misery as though it were our own.
Christ took his place with the condemned,
an innocent deliberately allowing Himself
to be arrested.
God's love gives everything, always.

Only the highest of convictions
causes a person to care
for the lowliest of people.

If we can't be responsive to the least among us,
how strong are we as a nation or community?

## *A Prophet*

Being a Christian means being a prophet—
and required to speak out against injustice.

Charity is no substitute for justice.

To say you don't know what to do for others
is to say you don't know who you are.
Not knowing what to do is a dodge.

Our good deeds illuminate God's presence
in the world.

Charity, sympathy, tolerance and understanding
(in a word: love)
are life-giving and signs of hope.

## *The Sunflower of the Soul*

Christ concealed his divinity and nobility.
He clothed his power in poverty.
We clothe our poverty in power.

We are shackled by fear, loneliness,
hatred, and egotism.
Christ came to liberate us . . .
so we in turn can liberate others.

The garden of solitude produces
many beautiful flowers,
the most beautiful of which is
compassion.

Compassion is the sunflower of the soul,
turning its face toward
the Son of God.

## *Be Not Afraid*

Be not afraid, the God of peace assures us.
Be not afraid of your weakness,
your inadequacy or your imperfection.
Love banishes fear.
God became weak and little,
a baby in need of help,
so we could face our own limitations
with faith and hope.

# PART THREE

# Terce

Let us bless
the Lord God living and true!
Let us always render Him
praise, glory, honor, blessing and every good.
Amen. Amen.
So be it. So be it.

Saint Francis of Assisi
—*Early Documents,* Volume I, page 141

# A Hidden Reality

*The innermost essence of God is hidden from us, totally separated from the created world. We can see hints of God's love, which is enduring and incomprehensible. God is utterly transcendent and lovingly immanent.*

*The call to holiness is an invitation to enter fully into a committed relationship with God. As we respond, God graciously nurtures growth in the relationship, by using events, circumstances, and people in our lives as instruments to hasten a contemplative outlook on life. Prayer becomes a vital part of our day; and, in prayer, we encounter more fully the Author of our life. This personal encounter with the Creator slowly transforms us into a Divine likeness, as it gently erases all traces of the un-God-like stuff within us. In prayer, we unlock the vault to our deepest self and allow light to shine on God who is already abiding at the very core of our being, hidden from us yet patiently waiting for us.*

## *A Gift*

Strive to live the present moment
as it truly is: a gift from God.

Every living thing should cause us to praise
the Creator of all living things.

Every event of our lives is open to God;
prayer reveals how.

The whole world, including every aspect of humanity,
is sacred and a gateway to God.

## *The Hidden Love of God*

Day in and day out,
God the divine Sower
liberally plants seeds
in the soil of our lives.
Prayer tills the soil,
making it receptive
to the flowering power of the seed.

But far too often
the soil is hardened
by sin, worries, and
an unhealthy preoccupation
with money, power, and success,
and so the seed
is trampled on or blown away.

We talk a lot about love,
but the concrete experience of love
is a rare thing indeed.

We claim God's love created the earth
and that same love appeared on earth
in Christ.
But we do not see it
or feel it.
God's love goes unnoticed.

To make visible the hidden love of God,
to feel more intensely
the inexpressible marvel of God,
we need to spend time in prayer
and time with the poor.

Because each of us is
a child of God,
each of us possesses the eminent dignity of
a child of God.

Divine mercy is incarnated
in human weakness.

### Prayer's Daughter

Prayer should lead us to
wholeness and simplicity.

Prayer quiets anger.

Gentleness is the daughter of prayer.

Love, detachment, and humility
form a triptych of the holy life.

### Sea of Love

The only thing worth learning is prayer.
Nothing else matters.

Only by entering fully and without reservation
into the infinite sea of Love
can we be transformed into the person
we were created to be.

Oh sweet Lord, I pray for the grace
to empty myself of all that is only me
so that I may be filled with what is only You.

### God and Servant

Prayer emerges naturally from silence.

Forgiveness must be exercised daily.

The gift of mercy must be shared.

Jesus took on the role of servant . . .
should we not do likewise?

Unconditional mercy requires total forgiveness
with absolutely no conditions.
To place conditions on mercy and forgiveness
is a form of violence.

### The Mystery Within

Our journey to God begins in earnest
when we still our senses, desires, and mind.
In stillness, real movement begins.

Within the silence of our hearts
lies a mystery beyond our hearts.

Only an open and serene heart
can absorb God's love.

Everyone has the potential to be a mystic—
to awaken to the deep mystery
within them and beyond them.
Mysticism is not relegated to a select few.

### Child of God

I am a child of God. Do I act like it?

God became like us
so we could become like God.

Imagine . . . you can hold in your very being
the One who holds the whole universe.
Amazing. True.

## Carrying the Cross of Others

The crucified and transfigured Christ's message of love
compels us to judge no one, to exclude no one;
moreover, it requires us to help others
to carry their cross,
fully sharing in their pain and suffering.

The incarnation of Christ epitomizes God's passion
for the poor and the disinherited.

When it comes to helping the poor,
we do not have to do everything.
But we do have to do everything we can.

## The Other

All of humanity is a single Person.

The diverse unity of humanity
is torn asunder by sin.

The Other is revealed in the face of the other.

## Stick 'Em Up

The incarnation and life and death of Christ
teaches not to place any limits on forgiveness
or on sharing.

My ego never tires of trying to rob me of my true self.

Prayer quiets negative passions.

Love is the only path to peace.

## *The Iron Fist*

Kindness refreshes and restores
the tired and broken.

Shared love leads to abundant life.

God wants us to see each other as tabernacles,
as secret hiding places for the Divine.
Pray for the grace to be able to see
a homeless person as a tabernacle of God.

The common good, which is the breath of freedom
and the social bond between people,
is being choked by the iron fist of individualism.

## *Sit Down and Rest*

When I deliberately put my whims
before the will of God by sinning
I get depressed over my failure to love
and subsequently my prayer life suffers.
But there is no reason for despair,
because God's mercy is boundless.

Sin blows out the flame of love for God
but God's mercy and forgiveness sets it aflame again.

God hates sin because of the harm it does to us,
but it is impossible for God
to hate us for our sins
because the essence of the Divine Being
is merciful love.

God's mercy is without limit.

## *The Wages of Sin*

Sin is not a private matter;
sin has a social dimension
because it causes estrangement
with our neighbor.

Sin blinds us
and renders us
incapable of spiritual perception.

The Gospel is not neutral.
It has strong, even radical,
opinions and ideas about everything,
especially sin.

When it comes to our sins,
we often make two mistakes,
both fatal to our spiritual life:
we either ignore them
or make excuses for them.
Our sins cannot be
ignored or excused.

## *A Life of Resistance*

We are being fed the lie
that individualism is the pinnacle
of human development.
Christ certainly did not believe that.

Competitive greed is not a natural part
of human nature.

Do not be conformed to the ways of the world,
the fashions of the hour.
The ways of God transcend
the ways of any society,
culture, or age.
To be a Christian means we must live
a life of resistance—resistance to sin,
compulsions, despair, injustice,
and the lies of popular culture.
To be a Christian, we must soak up
the grace that liberates us
from everything that holds us back
from unity with God.

We are prisoners of consumerism.

When my priorities revolve around
money and consumption,
I have no time to be
available to others—or God—and it will be
impossible to live a life of
surrender and service,
which is to say the life of
a Christian.

Simplicity is the key to unraveling
the complexities of modern life.

## A Deep Need

All addictions mask a craving
to be loved
and express a need
for acceptance or power.

The emptiness we feel
stems from not realizing
we are made for communion with God.
If we are not growing toward unity with God,
then we are growing apart from God.
We need to bring to Christ what we are,
so that in time we become what He is.

We all crave to be on the receiving end of
a gift of love;
but our very craving masks a deeper,
more profound human need:
to give love.

Breaking the bondage of egoism
is the toughest task in life.
Liberation is difficult and painful.

## A New Tune

The richness of God is revealed
in the poverty of Christ.

Is the sole reason for my living to do God's will?
It was Jesus' sole reason for living
and if I am a follower of His,
it must be mine also.
"My will be done" is still, sadly, my anthem.
I must sing a new tune.

When I have ceased to be important to myself,
the door to my soul is opened
for God to become important to me.

## A Few Dollars

The poor, the weak, and the hurting
are God in the flesh.

Service to the poor and lowly is not optional . . .
it is a requirement for the follower of Christ.

To turn your back on the poor
is to turn your back on Jesus.

Giving a few dollars to the poor
is not the same as being one with the poor,
which is what Christ requires.

The moral measure of any society or community
can be gauged by how it treats its weakest member.

## Rich in Mercy

To run from the experience of poverty
is to run from God.

I tell myself that I love God with all my heart,
but my actions reveal an insincerity
that borders on dishonesty.

What can I give to God?
Nothing . . . absolutely nothing.
Except for my trust and total self-surrender.

God's love for us does not cease or diminish
as a result of our sins, failures, or faults.
God is rich in mercy.

Jesus did not die on the cross
because he was angry at me.
He died on the cross
because he loves me.

For Jesus, the cross was where
love and forgiveness intersected.

## *The Poverty of Our Hearts*

God chooses to live in the poverty of our hearts.

Contemplation takes us out of the world
so we may see the world better, more clearly.

A life lived for God requires
living life as an offering . . .
a gift to be given away.

In word and deed,
Christ made it abundantly clear
that God prizes humility
and looks favorably on the humble.

### *Soul Mates*

Faith and justice are soul mates
whose hearts cry out for the poor.

The seduction of property
blinds us to the needs of the poor.

To forget the poor
is to forget God.

God did not create poverty.
People did.
And because people created poverty,
people can also end it.

Chronic poverty is as great a scandal
as terrorism, and it needs
to be tackled with similar urgency.
Terrorism flourishes in nations
that fail to lift people out of poverty.

### *No Excuse*

From God's point of view,
true success in human life
is measured
by your ability to
incarnate the beatitudes.

If the Gospel is not about love and justice,
it has been reduced to mere sentimentality.

When it comes to helping the poor,
not knowing what to do
is not an excuse not to do anything.
Do what you can.

## A Place to Sleep

Jesus embraced simplicity, poverty, and humility.
What do we embrace?

God hides in a piece of broken bread
and in the broken life of a slum-dweller.

The life of Christ makes it clear
that God chooses humility over majesty,
that infinity dwells in the finite.

While God's love embraces all people,
God has clearly demonstrated deep concern
for the poor and the needy,
the helpless and the oppressed.
God demands that we side with the poor,
the powerless, and victims of injustice.
To walk with the poor
is to be in harmony with the will of God.

Justice requires that all people
have a place to sleep, enough food to eat,
and work that makes them feel worthwhile.

## One Body

The enemy in our battle to overcome
chronic, unjust poverty
is our misguided spirit of individualism . . .
our snobbery, apathy, prejudice, and blind unreason.
Though we are many,
we are one body in the eyes of God,
all animated by one Spirit.
And as members of one body
we each have a responsibility
for one another.

We cannot separate justice and charity . . .
they must go together, hand-in-hand,
in order to solve the problem created
by chronic poverty.

## Holding Something Back

Being selfish is exhausting.
Being selfless is refreshing.

The ego is the source of pain.
God is the source of life.
God and ego cannot occupy
the same throne in your life.

No matter how grave or slight,
all sin is in the will.
It is a deliberate choice
not to give God everything.

## Hot Pursuit

We must be on guard
not to confuse the necessities of life
with what is luxurious.
The humble simplicity
that embodies poverty of spirit
stands in stark contrast
to the unbridled pursuit of
comfort, power, pleasure, and riches,
which permeate a society
that prizes possession as a good in itself.

Poverty of spirit is a humble, little room
where infinite mystery
encounters concrete existence.
It is a room where we can
empty ourselves
in order to be filled
with God.

Poverty of spirit animates a life of generosity.
We can be generous with all we possess
because our real treasure is
nothing less than union with God.

Renunciation, paradoxically, is the best path
to liberation.

### *The Detached Heart*

Seeing my own weaknesses clearly enables me
to acknowledge my own poverty
and my need for God.

When you forget yourself,
God remembers you.

In emptiness we shall find fullness.

The detached heart knows the fullness
of peace, joy, and freedom,
and sees the face of God
illuminated in all of creation.

## Reality?

Our desires distort our perception of reality.

Our emotions and desires create
our reality and shape our lives.

Whatever you care about most
will determine the course of your life.

## At the End of My Rope

Perhaps God brings us to the end of our resources
so we can discover the vastness of His.

Our spiritual life will not prosper
without an intense awareness
of our own poverty and emptiness.

Unity with God is obtained in only one way:
total surrender.

## Broken and Restored

In the state of emptiness,
you are better able to encounter
the fullness of God.

No one is self-sufficient.
We need others and the Other.

Only when I am vulnerable
is it possible for me to be broken
and restored to the image of God.

## *The Boob Tube*

The commercial advertisements that fuel television
deliver one common message:
do not be satisfied with what you have—
only more "stuff" can make you happy.

Spiritual reading gives me the chance
to spend time with remarkable men and women
who have looked long and lovingly at the Real.


## *You First*

Jesus instructed us never to think of ourselves
as more important than others,
never to put ourselves before anyone.
His message is clear:
think little of yourself
and be happy that others
do not consider you very important.
Moreover, Jesus asks us to stop struggling
to control events for our own benefit,
and instead try to be a servant to others.
Sadly, I find it easy to ignore His advice.

Self-importance fosters an addiction
to and craving for human respect.

I am the source of my own misery.
As my ego decreases,
happiness and peace increases.

It is impossible to be filled with the spirit of God
if we are filled with ourselves.
Surrender precedes the indwelling presence
of the Spirit.

## *The Road Less Traveled*

When we realize the emptiness of
all material things,
we are free to encounter God.

All that is "self" must be abandoned
if we are to follow Jesus.
The road He travels
is the road of self-emptying.

When profit is the aim and law of life,
then humanity suffers a great loss.


## *What?*

Without silence,
we are deaf.

Our real pilgrimage is into
the depths of silence . . .
and leads to a true light.

I cannot provide light for myself.
Light is a gift that
needs to be received.

Empty your heart;
sit in stillness.

Quiet your fears;
rest in God.

## *Unending Mercy*

My faults and failures remind me
of the unending mercy of God.

God loves us because
we need to be loved.

Forgiveness gives birth to love
and destroys enmity.

All we can give God
is our needs.

A thankful heart
is a patient heart.

## *A Hard Time*

God's love and mercy are far greater
than my countless infidelities
and my inability to totally surrender my will.
Thank God.

God grant me the grace
to truly feel my intrinsic poverty.

We have become so separated
from the poor and the suffering
that we have lost the chance
to find true fulfillment by giving of ourselves.

If I require security,
I will have a hard time feeling true compassion
for the poor and the weak.

## The Whole Universe

The beginning of peacemaking
is the ability to say God loves me . . .
and I love myself.

To be at peace with yourself
is to be at peace
with the whole universe.

Life, at its core, is an act of communion.

Without listening, it is impossible to know God
—or peace.


## God's Will

Shared love leads to abundant life.

Compassion is far removed
from pity and sympathy.
Compassion grows out of an awareness
of our common humanity.

What is God's will?
Simple: love, mercy,
justice, healing,
peace, and forgiveness.

To share is to break the bread of our lives . . .
to give our hearts, our hopes,
our dreams, our thoughts, our time.

## Old Ways

Let go of old thoughts and ideas,
old ways of thinking,
and put on the mind of Christ
in order to see as God sees.

Living more deeply within
eventually causes a person
to live more simply without.

Jesus was born in poverty and simplicity.
How can I reject (or dishonor)
the birthplace of my savior.


## A Journey to Weakness

Spirituality is essentially a journey
in which we move from what we are
to what we will be;
it is a journey to weakness.
We truly learn to live when we begin
to explore our weaknesses.
Every experience of weakness
is an opportunity of growth and renewed life.
Weaknesses transformed by the reality of Christ
become life-giving virtues.

Everything that happens to us—
both good and bad,
the joys and sorrows,
the success and failures—
fuels our spiritual progress.
Everything draws us to God—
if we allow it.

Even our sins can be used by God
to help us abandon ourselves
and respond to God's love.

Thank God we do not have to save ourselves,
do not have to make ourselves pleasing
in the eyes of God.

### *Walk with Christ*

Christ liberates me from the burden
of being the boss.

Christ wants us to be
more and more free of fear
so we may become
more and more capable of love.

To worship Christ without actively participating
in His life, suffering, and death
is just another form of idolatry.
It is easier to worship Christ
than to stand with Him
in His struggle against sin, hatred, and injustice.
Christ needs followers, not just worshippers.

When we choose the cross,
we choose to join the struggle of the oppressed.

Don't admire Christ; walk with Christ.

When we walk with Christ,
everything that happens to us
can be converted into good,
into a magnet that draws us closer to God.

## *Human Form*

God's will for each of us
is that we live lives of unselfish charity.

We need to find ourselves
and give ourselves away.

Every day God comes to us
in human form—and we turn our back.

Every act of mercy and kindness
brings us closer to the reality of God.

We all have the same vocation:
a life of holiness.
But there are countless ways for each of us
to individually and uniquely animate
the love of God.

## *A Lifelong Pilgrimage*

I cannot learn about God.
I can only unlearn the things
that are keeping me
from a full awareness of God.

Our reason can only lead us
to knowledge about God,
not to God.

To find Christ you must make a pilgrimage
to the center of your being,
to the place where the human and the divine meet.

The key to being a pilgrim
is to remain interiorly still as you journey . . .
otherwise you are just a wanderer.

To pray is to embark on a journey without end—
a journey deep into the heart of darkness, of paradox,
of mystery.

The journey to God is slow.
Each day, we inch our way along a steep, winding road.
The pace of spiritual transformation
moves about as quickly as traffic in Los Angeles.

# A Knapsack and Walking Stick

*St. Francis of Assisi said, "When the brothers go through the world, let them take nothing for the journey, neither knapsack nor purse, nor bread, nor money, nor walking stick."*

*As we conclude this second Hour, it is good to realize we are on a journey, a journey to God. What are we taking with us? Me . . . I'm lugging a lot of stuff, far more than can fit in a knapsack. Mostly, I am carrying my sins. They slow me down.*

*But slowly as I travel I am learning to see that my sins do not erase from my soul the fundamental dignity that God stamped on it at my conception. God does not want to see my demise. God's mercy continuously desires to give me new life. Sin alienates me from God. But God does not reject me because of my sin. God simply wants me to refrain from sinning, because my sins prevent me from experiencing the love God wants to shower upon me.*

*For so long, I thought my sins were beyond redemption. They had me bound so tightly, it was impossible to free myself from their choking control. But I did not understand the power of grace. I underestimated the unlimited power of God.*

*Dimly, I am beginning to see that God can overcome my personal weakness. All I have to do is let Him. But before God can work, I must wake up and admit I need God's help. Genuine, sincere contrition is always fully embraced by God's tender loving mercy.*

*Lord Jesus Christ, have mercy on me a sinner.*

*As I journey through life, that simple phrase is constantly on my lips. The more I repeat it, the more profound its truth.*

*Lord Jesus Christ, have mercy on me a sinner.*

# PART FOUR

# Sext

Almighty, eternal, just and merciful God,
give us miserable ones
the grace to do for You alone
what we know you want us to do
and always to desire what pleases You.
Inwardly cleansed,
interiorly enlightened
and inflamed by the fire of the Holy Spirit,
may we be able to follow
in the footprints of Your beloved Son,
our Lord Jesus Christ,
and, by Your grace alone,
may we make our way to You,
Most High,
Who live and rule
in perfect Trinity and simple Unity,
and are glorified
God almighty,
forever and ever.
Amen.

St. Francis of Assisi
—*Early Documents*, Volume I, pages 121-122

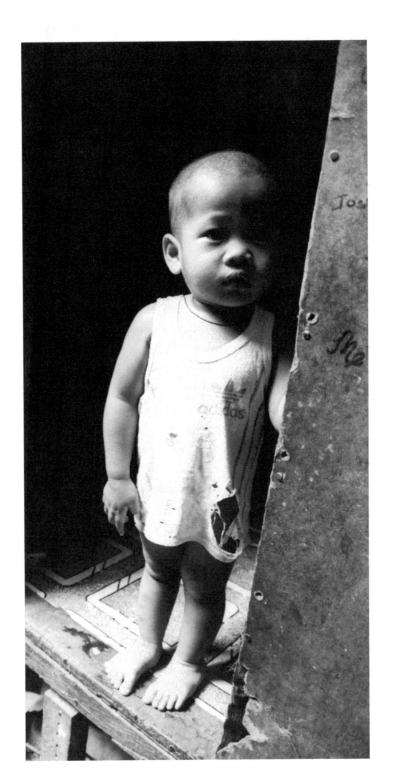

# Merciful Love

*Reliance upon your own determined efforts to achieve sanctity is doomed to failure. While acts of virtue are important, holiness actually has more to do with receiving than giving. It is a pure gift from God, given freely to all those who humbly ask for it, accepting everything in their lives as grace. God's merciful love is far greater than our most valiant acts of virtue. Confidence in God's merciful love is vital; it allows you to surrender your entire life, with all its layers of imperfections, to God, allowing God's merciful love full reign to make all things new. Confidence in God's merciful love gives you the freedom to love your own lack of power, because you know that no matter how often you stumble, fall, and fail, God is there to help you up. God seeks empty hands. Empty hands allow God to give you everything you need.*

## Help Me

Lord, I ask you this day for one thing:
give me the grace to live
a clean and transparent life,
both internally and externally.
Help me be good,
merciful, thankful, and patient.

It is not enough to pray.
One must be prayer incarnate.

## The Road to Holiness

The road to holiness is paved
with authentic penance.

Humility is fundamental to holiness.

Humility teaches me to be attentive to others.

## Child of God

Sometimes it takes courage to believe
you are better than you feel,
that you are a child of God.

Admit your weaknesses
and bravely face your challenges.

I am not God, but I am a child of God.

Boldly be what God wants you to be.

It pleases God to do what is good for you.

If you can manage to cooperate with grace,
your life will be full, whole.

## No Illusions

God wants us to give up our illusions.
We hate this.
We like pretending
that good is within our reach.

God is not asking us to become perfect;
God is asking us to surrender everything.

Self-abandonment is a continual forgetting of one's self
in order to constantly remember God.

God seeks intimacy.

The surest way to experience
intimacy with God
is to jettison everything
that does not lead to God.

## Alive and Loving

Holiness and justice go hand-in-hand.

Without the hope that God is God,
alive and loving,
injustice grows easily.

To whitewash injustice is in itself an injustice.

The devil loves violence . . .
because it disrupts and violates peace.

A child of God must become
a parent of justice and peace.

The hallmarks of authentic humanity
are love and justice.

## *The Cloud of Unknowing*

My greatest challenge:
make the invisible reality of God visible.

The widespread suffering caused by injustice
is ample proof that most people
do not really believe in God.
True belief in God would demand
we end all suffering caused by injustice.

Wisdom is being comfortable in the midst
of change and uncertainty;
it is content under
the cloud of unknowing.

The pursuit of power and independence
is counterproductive to spiritual growth,
unless it is able to be transformed into love.

Love is the ultimate vulnerability.

Knowledge is useless
without love.

## *The Splendor of Goodness*

God shines through all of creation.

Creation shimmers with the splendor of goodness,
revealing endless reflections
of the Trinity.

## *Tough Message*

Grace is God's way of talking to us.
We can best experience grace
and therefore hear God more clearly
when we stop living for ourselves
and instead give ourselves
in loving service to others.

Christ's message can be reduced to this:
make every stranger,
no matter how poor or dirty,
no matter how weak or unlovable,
your neighbor.
Tough message.

Am I a sacrament of salvation for my neighbor?

Terrorism, no matter how abhorrent and brutal,
does not render the Gospel irrelevant.
We are called to love our enemies.
Christ is the center of all things;
He holds all things together in love.

With hardly a hint of protest
we allowed liberty and justice
to become
shock and awe.

While we wage war
for oil,
Millions are dying from
a lack of water.

Christ does not defeat our enemies;
he asks us to pray for them.

### The Imitation of Christ

Weary are my days
when I crave God and resist God
at the same time . . .
which I do nearly everyday.

All God wants is a surrendered heart.

The road to God takes us through
conversion, contrition, and communion.
And it does so on a daily basis.

The desire to imitate Christ
is the first step in actually doing so.

Can I trace Christ-like patterns in my life?

How quickly our "hosannas" of Palm Sunday
turn into Good Friday cries
of "Crucify him."

Our sins shout, "Crucify him."


### I Am the Resurrection

The resurrection is not reserved for the future.
The resurrection needs to happen here and now.

We must share in the resurrection every day.

We have forgotten the resurrection
and its life-transforming power.

For the most part, Christians have changed
their religion
instead of changing the world.
Christianity has essentially become
a private and individual affair.

And the Christian, in most cases,
is only interested in his or her
own suffering and resurrection.

Liberation is found only in the resurrection.


## *Awake and Aware*

The love of God leads us somewhere—
we just do not know where.
We have no choice
but to follow God into the unknown.

Give your heart eyes,
alert eyes,
eyes wide open
to the presence of God.

The unhealthy habits of our hearts
hinder our ability to embrace God.

The biggest obstacle to prayer
is the way we pray,
trying to verbalize everything.
Effective prayer goes beyond words and images;
it requires a complete awareness
of the present moment.

Stay awake and aware . . .
open to the present moment.

### Beyond Our Grasp

God is a God of self-giving
and we experience the self-gift
only dimly and incompletely.

We cannot comprehend the God
upon whom we depend.

Ceaseless questioning about what life means
is an essential part of being a human being.
The answer, however, is always
beyond our grasp.

Faith is permanently growing,
always in process.


### Starry Night

Jesus was a poet
of his own internal experience.

If your faith cannot be woven into
the mundane stuff of everyday life and activities,
it is not a living faith.

God is nearer than we imagine.
Begin your search for God
in the ordinary and familiar.

God can be found in your garden,
in your attic, and in the grocery store.
God is in a summer breeze
and the beauty of a starry night.

## *Endowed with Nobility*

God dwells in every human.
Every human is endowed with a nobility
that stems from the reality
that we are created in the image of God.

This nobility entitles each of us
to a capacity for union
with the infinite love of God.

Sin prevents us from seeing
all of humanity
as our family,
preventing us from relating
to one another
as sister and brother.

## *The Humanity of God*

God thinks about us,
so we can think about God.
This is the essence of love,
forgetting yourself
and thinking about
the object of your love.

God needs to be the total content of one's life.

God manifests Himself in everything.
Most of the time, we just do not see it.

The humanity of God
is transparent in all people.

I am a manifestation
of the humanity of God.

### *Loving Eyes*

Being correct
is not the same as
being in love.

When you see Christ in a person,
you cannot look on that person
with lust, envy, or anger in your eyes.
You look at the person through loving eyes.

A capacity for the Infinite was woven
into the heart of every human being
by the Creator.

Those who formed me,
by their words and actions,
are part of who I am.

### *Little Gestures*

Love is for giving and forgiving.

Our greatest violation of poverty
is to hold the good God gives;
goodness has to flow.

Love is made visible
in the little gestures of our lives.

Acts of charity are the wings of Love.

All good must be given back to God.

## A New Creation

Trials and temptations
are God's way of showing us
the broken nature of humanity.

Christ does not relieve our pain;
He enters it with us.

The mystery of the incarnation
deals with the stuff of life—
and the choices we make.

Incarnation transforms us by grace,
changing us into
what we were made to be: LOVE.

All creation is in the state of evolution,
in the state of becoming.

Only love can fix
our broken world.

We are instruments of incarnation . . .
calling forth a new creation.

We become mothers of incarnation
by giving birth to the Word of God
by the way we live and work.

God is with us . . . every moment of every day.
If we forget that, we are doomed.

## Crucified Love

God pursues us
more than we pursue God.
Infinitely more.

Our longing for God is weak and easily distracted.

God, whose richness knows no limitation,
has chosen to enter into our poverty.

The Cross demonstrates the depths of God's love.

The crucified Love of God
is our gate to peace and freedom.

## Rejected Love

Freedom is a gift of God's love.

God has deliberately exposed Himself
to the perils of our rebelliousness.

God's love is constantly rejected
and yet God continues to love.

God's omnipotence has a self-imposed impotence.
God cannot force humans to love.
We can thwart the fulfillment of creation
by excluding God from it.
We have been given extraordinary freedom.

God gives us the freedom to reject God;
and it is that very freedom
which allows us to love God.

## The School of Life

The mystery of the Incarnation
leads us to recognize that our relationship
with each other and with the mystery of God
is shaped and learned and lived in time.

Life is a school.
And spiritual communion
is its main lesson.

Our love of God can be measured
by our love for one another.

We must worship God
with more than our lips.
We must worship God
with our hearts and lives also.

## Self-Giving Love

Suffering is a lack of something
that makes us whole, complete.
Our lack of health, respect, and resources
blocks us from being whole.

Suffering and death are part
of the evolutionary process.

God did not chose to eliminate suffering.
God has chosen to enter into suffering.
We wish God had chosen differently.

We are in a dynamic process of self-transcendence.

God's power is in self-giving love.

## New Life

God pours His self-emptying love
into unlimited acts of mercy
wherein He eagerly shares in our sufferings.
God's mercy heals and renews us,
gives us new life.
God's mercy is strong and steadfast
in its embrace of sinners,
absorbing our suffering
and helping us carry the weight of our misdeeds.

God's mercy inspires the sinner
to change.

Without God's mercy
I would quickly wither and die.
And if I do not share God's mercy
with those around me,
with all those in need of mercy and forgiveness,
then I am guilty of hoarding
the transforming power of mercy for myself.

Divine mercy must flow
through one human toward other humans.

True contemplation helps one heal the hurts
of others.
Contemplation leads to compassion.

The more of God's merciful love we receive,
the more compelled we are
to extend an offering of mercy to others.

## *The Seat of Sadness*

We sin not because we are bad;
we sin because we are weak.

Our sinfulness, no matter how bad,
never puts us outside of God's love.
We pay for our sinfulness here and now
because sin prevents us
from truly enjoying anything.

Sin robs us of true and lasting joy.
Sin is the seat of sadness.

Sin breeds cynicism.

Our sins are compounded
when we deny or excuse them,
because when we deny or rationalize sinful behavior
we hinder our ability to experience
God's unmerited mercy and forgiveness.

## *A Life of Childlike Vulnerability*

Self-righteous judgment of others
is based on fear and ignorance.

When we have felt
the embrace of God's love
we are no longer unwilling
to embrace others.

When we are filled with God's boundless love,
we have no other choice
but to be endless mercy to all.
Cloaked in God's protective and nourishing love,
we are free to live a life of childlike vulnerability.

## Seeing Everything Differently

We were created to love God.
But because of sin,
we love created things
more than the Creator.
And so we live in disharmony,
with each other and God.

My sin does not make me contemptible.
My sin cannot destroy the dignity
with which God has crowned humanity.

Faith allows us to gently touch
the mystery of life,
the mystery of God.
Faith allows us to see
everything differently.
Faith senses the presence of God
in everything.
Faith makes everything beautiful.

## Inner Disunity

Fear and sin are siblings.

Even my sin cannot separate me from God,
because there is no separation
between ourselves and God.

Sin is our attempt to grab something
we feel we lack.

Lust seeks a forceful union with another
in order to compensate
for the inner disunity we feel.

God accepts our humanity—why can't we?

## The Ultimate Darkness

God gives me life
yet I evade God.
Every day I am graced
and yet sinful.

Prayer brings us face to face with
the ultimate darkness.
Prayer challenges us to enter the darkness
or turn away from it.

In the darkness I am able to see
my own insecurity.
In the darkness I learn I need light
from Someone else.

## Fractured by Sin

Salvation is not in the future.
Salvation is in the past, our past.
We find salvation by returning
to the unity in which we were created.
Our salvation is merely a re-integration
of unity with God
and all of creation,
a unity which has been fractured by sin,
by our living out of our inner brokenness
which causes deeper disunity.

## *Guard Duty*

Strength without humility
is useless and impotent.

Our lack of humility is the result of our dishonesty.
We exaggerate our self-importance
and our achievements,
and distort the truth about
our real impoverishment and sinfulness.

If Jesus was poor and humble, shouldn't we be also?

Be ever conscious of your deficiency and helplessness.
Pray for grace.

Arrogance and pride peddle the lie
that we do not need to pray.

Moderate your pleasures; practice self-denial.

Guard your senses;
they are portals
through which sin can enter the soul.

## *Puffed Up*

Humility reflects the spirituality of the cross—
Christ descending to earth.

Do not rush to the highest place;
take the lowest place, voluntarily.

The last place is the best place.

Become little.

Do not become proud, puffed up.

Humility is the bread and butter of the spiritual life.

Humility is a practical way to share
in the passion of Christ.
Humility is part of loving your brother and sister,
because humility allows me to love
the goodness within others,
and helps me put them ahead of myself.

## Meek and Humble

Humility is the cornerstone of repentance.
Sadly, humility's stock has declined in our time.
Instead, we value a sense of pride,
a sense of self-glorification,
a sense of self-righteousness.
Today, many people view humility
as a sign of weakness.
How easily we forget the words of Christ:
"Learn from me for I am meek and humble in heart."

Repentance, deeply rooted in humility,
is a return to the right order of things.
Repentance is the path out of exile.

Repentance is more than "pleading guilty"
to transgressions.
Repentance needs to acknowledge
our alienation from God,
our failure to enter fully into the joy
of communion with the Divine.
Repentance is not merely a response
to a spiritual indictment;
it must also be a response to the fact
that we have strayed from the glory of God.

## *Our Inner Cravings*

Unmindful consumption is a sure path
to suffering.

By moving through and beyond suffering
we enter into the freedom of God.

In silence we become aware
that we may have wandered off the path
to the inner freedom produced by a God-centered life.
In silence we turn around
and find our way back to the true path.

In silence we are able to hear our inner cravings
and recognize the pain caused by
our separation from God.

## *Creative Silence*

Silence produces an inner restfulness
that helps the soul to soar.
The greatest malady of our time
is the absence of stillness and silence.

Silence gives us space for receptivity;
it allows us to hear the speechless language of God
and to respond with our hearts.

To become more and more silent,
to enter deeply into creative silence, takes courage.
The wordless is foreign to us.
Yet God transcends language and intellect.

Only in silence can you hear the vast, boundless depths
of the Spirit speaking more and more clearly
about the unlimited love and mercy of God.
Be still. Be quiet. Be.

### The Language of Silence

Truth and serenity lie sleeping
in silence and solitude.

Life emerges in the darkness and silence of the womb.

Silence is the soil of renewal.

Silence is the language of God.

### Silently Speaking

We shout. God whispers.

God works in silence.

Without voice, God silently speaks
in and through everything.

### Authentic Transformation

Outside the inevitable suffering
caused by death and accidents,
most suffering bubbles up out of
our craving for transitory things
and our worldly attachments.

It is easy to become attached
to the kind of secure certainty
peddled by religious fundamentalism.
But this kind of "knowing"
is a roadblock to true knowing.
Clinging to the comfort of certainty
is just as bad as all our temporal attachments.

It is difficult for God's Word to enter
our inner temple
because its entrance is blocked

by our endless array of attachments.
In order to be heard,
God requires silence and detachment from us.

Without daily contemplative silence
it is impossible to have
a true encounter with God's Word within us,
where authentic transformation begins.

### Poor and Pardoned

Jesus never promised security . . .
yet that is what we seek.

I am poor and pardoned.
Nothing more.

Poverty of spirit does not refer
to an economic condition.
It reflects the human reality
that we are poor before God
and, consequently, we need
to radically depend on God alone
for true fulfillment.

### The Bread of Life

Almsgiving is not charity, it is justice.

Unbind the poor—
the physically poor and the spiritually poor—
and give them something to eat—
either bread or the Bread of Life.

We have the means to feed everyone on earth.
We do not have the will to do it.
This is a tremendous evil.

### *Buyer Beware*

Today's new religion
—consumerism—
has one basic creed:
having is more important than being.

Success today is gauged by how much you can buy.

Happiness cannot be hinged to having.

You don't need mercy and grace
when you can buy anything you want.
Consumerism is slowly and softly killing
the human spirit,
destroying human dignity.

A life that finds its expression in consuming
is not capable of compassion.

The experience of grace has been diminished
by the rising lust for accumulating and devouring.

### *Not Mine*

Ownership is an illusion.
I really can't own anything.
God owns everything.
The word "mine"
diminishes the Lordship of God.

Everything belongs to God.

I only own my sins and vices
because they do not come from God.

## Core Values

Faith is more important than self-reliance.

A religion that is not reverent is not relevant.

Your core values tell others what is important to you.

Our values influence our behavior.

The study of theology is important.
But theology should never trump
prayer and devotion.

## An Unfettered Mind

The less you have,
the less you have to distract you
from God.

To become poor is to know
the richness of God.

The danger of building up riches
is that an accumulation of wealth
makes it easy to succumb
to a self-complacency
that makes God superfluous.

Without clinging to anything,
we must patiently stand before God
with open hands.

Jesus is not asking us to get rid of our possessions;
he is asking us to lose our attachment to them.
He knows an unfettered mind is essential
to entering the emptiness
where God can meet us.

## Grabbing It All

The impulse to accumulate all we can
needs to be thwarted.
We have no right
to own more than we need.
And we need far less
than we want.

Voluntary physical poverty is a means
to a healthy spiritual poverty.

Exterior and interior poverty are close friends.

A spirit of poverty makes detachment
from possessions possible.
Poverty of spirit
fights the instinct to possess.

Gratification of the instinct to possess
material things
makes one susceptible to the vice of selfishness—
grabbing all you can for yourself,
without regard for others.

## Thank You

During the Eucharistic celebration we say,
"It is fitting and right to give thanks."
Thankfulness is the door to the Kingdom of God.
The first and last words of our day
should be "thank you."
All life is a gift from God,
which we in turn must give away.

The two most important words
of any prayer are: thank you.

Gratitude to God unleashes enough divine energy
to move mountains.

A grateful heart is a joyful heart.
And a joyful heart is a creative heart,
finding new ways to give itself away.

# A Gift of Love

*The end of isolation is found in prayer. Through prayer, we become aware that God is present. Through prayer we become at home with the living presence with whom we can share everything. And in the presence of God we become aware of our complete dependence on the Creator. Prayer fosters within us a spirit of humility and the realization that we cannot truly live without God.*

*Prayer is a gift of Love, and a means of living our whole life as a communion with the Lord who, through the Incarnation, came to share in our human conditions. As we encounter God in the depths of ourselves, we are no longer astonished by the darkness of God's mystery, but we merely accept it, living by faith. We no longer belong to ourselves but to Love, the giver of the gift. When we enter fully into the presence, we experience spontaneous joy . . . even during trials, hardships, and suffering. Even when we are weak, empty, and hurting, we know the Lord is present. Trusting in this presence we are compelled to accept everything as coming from God.*

# PART FIVE

# None

A pilgrim while in his body, away from the Lord,
Francis, the man of God,
strove to keep himself present in spirit in heaven,
and, being already a fellow-citizen of the angels,
he was separated from them
only by the wall of the flesh.
With all his soul he thirsted for his Christ:
to him he dedicated not only his whole heart
but also his whole body.

He turned all his time into a holy leisure
in which to engrave wisdom on his heart,
so that, if he did not always advance,
he would not seem to give up.
If visits from people of the world
or any kind of business intruded,
he would cut them short,
rather than finish them,
and hurry back to the things that are within.
The world had no flavor to him,
fed on the sweetness of heaven,
and divine delicacies had spoiled him
for crude human fare.
He always sought out a hidden place
where he could join to God
not only his spirit
but every member of his body.

Thomas of Celano, *The Second Life of St. Francis*
—*Early Documents,* Volume II, pages 308-309

# Empty Pleasures

*To be a saint is to be fully human and fully aware that true happiness comes from God alone.*

*Each day I must confront the countless desires that rise up within me. And each day I must admit that I am powerless to satisfy those desires. Moreover, I must focus on the fact that all desires are fulfilled only in God. The deepest and most essential longing we have, no matter how hidden or misunderstood, is a longing for God. That longing, that call to holiness, is woven into the fabric of our existence. Each day, I need to affirm my dependence on God alone.*

*Unhealthy desires are extinguished by humility. See your nothingness; forget your self, and live for God and your neighbor.*

*Oh God, help me stop my restless searching for empty pleasures, which, even when satisfied, leave me feeling unsatisfied, leave me with a void that can only be filled by You.*

## The Sunrise of the Soul

Prayer slows down the frenzied pace of life.

Prayer prompts us to reach out in compassion
to the suffering and weak,
and helps us embrace all of humanity.

Prayer is the sunrise of the soul.

## In the Silence between Night and Day

As each new day dawns,
God's light gives us
a renewed pledge of God's love,
a fresh beginning that is pure gift,
a gift meant to be given away during the day.

In the silence between night and day,
we feel God's grace and peace
and are commissioned to become instruments
of that very same grace and peace.
In the splendor of new light,
God's love and mercy are revealed.

O God help us see the radiance of your light
and show us this day
how to be servants of your peace.

## *Weapons of Mass Distraction*

At the dawn of the new century
our spiritual lives are threatened
by countless weapons of mass distraction,
such as: mass media, cell phones, the internet,
near-constant noise, and obsessive consumerism.
So much of modern life
drives us from what is
most true and essential.
The way to disarm these deadly weapons
is simple:
prayer, fasting, and concern for those in need.

The intensity of TV and movie action and violence
creates within us an artificial poverty of experience,
making our everyday "real" lives
seem pallid and insignificant,
requiring artificial stimulation and addiction
in order to endure it.

The actual poverty of life
reveals our need for
the kind of abundant life
promised by Jesus.
It recently dawned on me
that my spiritual life has grown more steadily
as my movie viewing declined.

Life without solitude is a life out of balance.
We need to do more than
squeeze moments of solitude
out of our increasingly frenetic days.
Patches of seclusion
soothe the soul.

## *Hurt on Top of Hurt*

God does not dole out punishment.
We do.

God is aware of the hurt we feel before we sin,
the hurt which caused us to sin.
God does not wish to heap
more hurt on top of that hurt
by punishing us.
We are doing a fine job of that all by ourselves.

When we sin, we are trying to bury ourselves
because we do not like who we are.

God saves sinners.
Punishment is not part of the equation.

The devil is the manifestation of our temptation
toward self-destruction.

Surrender is never easy.
When Jesus was called to his final surrender
on the cross,
he sweat blood.


## *I Have Sinned*

The first step on the road of Christianity
is repentance.

Essentially, Christianity is about reconciliation.

God's mercy is always there to pick us up
and dust us off.

More than enshrining saints,
the Church needs to embrace sinners.

## Inner Demons

No one is untouched by
fears, neuroses, and anxieties.
Unless they are brought into the light,
they are free to terrorize us.

Life is all about healing oneself.

Face your shadow,
confront your inner demons.

We tend to deny in the darkness
what we experienced in the light.

## Nonstop

The consumer society we live in is nothing new.
Since the Fall, humans have been consuming
one another without pause.

Sin gives us a license to devour each other.

Sin diminishes our capacity to love.

Our "stuff" walls us off
from others,
preventing us from becoming
sister and brother
to all of creation,
including the poor souls
living on the margins of society.

## *My Comfort Zone*

From Christ's point of view,
"you" comes before "me."

The danger of our thirst for individualism
is that it weakens our awareness
of the needs of others.

A heart beating with compassion
is the primary fruit
of an encounter with the Cross.

The gift of faith is often rejected by Christians
who become too accustomed to their comfort,
too comfortable in their certainty about God.


## *Excuses*

Oh how easily we compromise our sin,
make excuses for it,
become comfortable with it.
And when we do so,
we compound and deepen our sin.

Prayer is the only weapon we need.


## *Glittering Radiance*

The harsh and frightening realities
of sickness, hunger, suffering and death
cover the earth, plaguing all its inhabitants,
each of whom is crying out
for the eager embrace of God's love.
But we do not have to wait.

God's loving arms are
always open and welcoming.
All we need to do
is turn toward God
and accept the divine hug
that awaits us.

In the glittering radiance of God's light,
chaos and darkness
take flight.

## Always Working

During those times when I am unable
to perceive the richness of God,
I become more aware of my incapacity and poverty.
God seems to occasionally withdraw
a sense of divine affection from me
in order for me to see the need
for ongoing conversion
and to always seek to increase
my spirit of purity and detachment.

God wants more than our hearts and minds,
more than our prayers and work.
God desires our entire being.

God never changes.
It is we who change.
And we change many times in any given day.
I can be fervent one moment
and discouraged the next.
Change is part of being human.
But God's goodness is constant and unchanging.
God is always working to draw us
more fully into Love.

During times of emptiness and sadness,
times of anguish and pain,
God is drawing us into
the Garden of Gethsemani,
inviting us to unite with
the agony of Christ.

## The Great Escape

Recognized or not, the greatest reality in life
is our desire to know and be united with God.
Sadly, our natural desire for God
has been so distorted by false desires
that we must purify from our hearts
before we can come close to God.

Our primary call is to stand before God
in a stance of conversion.

I need to escape from the distorting influences
of society
by checkering my life with periodic periods
of solitude.
Only solitude allows me to reconnect
with the truth
of my own nature and my relationship with God.

## The Root of Violence

Fear is the root of violence.

Only love overcomes fear.

The only response to violence is forgiveness.

Peace is the fruit of forgiveness.

Most of our problems stem
from our inability to forgive—
ourselves and others.

When you live in the heart of peace,
everything you encounter turns to good.

Behind every act of violence,
there is pain,
the pain of a wounded heart.

## Emptiness

Friendship requires listening.
Listening requires openness.
Openness requires faith.
Faith requires presence.
Presence requires being.
Being requires love.
Love requires emptiness.

## Death Sentence

Greed is a death sentence to the spirit.

When I am busy tending to the task
of providing for my own security,
I am not free to be sensitive
to the needs of others.

The cure for unjust material poverty is holiness.

The highest goodness contains
a quality of self-giving
that enriches both the giver and the receiver.

## *Spirit and Fire*

It is so easy to get caught up
in the do's and don'ts
of the morally correct life
that we forget the most important aspect
of our spiritual life:
growing in intimacy with God.

We have allowed Christianity
to be reduced to moralism,
and as a result we have become blind
to the creative presence of the Holy Spirit.

The Spirit anoints each of us
with a special gift,
that is revealed through
prayer and attentiveness.

Ancient Syrian Orthodox liturgies
describe the Eucharist as "spirit and fire."
How do you describe the Eucharist?

Look closely at the Eucharistic Liturgy
and you will see Christ praying.


## *A Two-Lane Highway*

Good deeds alone will not reverse our
sinful inclinations.
Human goodness alone does not grant us peace.
We need to surrender our hearts to God,
who Alone can free us from the urge to sin
and lead us to a peace which passes all understanding.

The road to authentic peace is a two-lane highway:
one lane is dedicated to surrendering to God's will,
and the other lane requires living in God's love.

### Slow Down

The sooner you slow down,
the quicker you will start living.

The desert is a place of contemplation,
not discovery.

Fasting feeds the soul.

Love, compassion, justice, and gratitude
are essential components of worship.

### Hard Work

If your spiritual life is not growing, it is declining.

The Christian life cannot be put on cruise control.
It takes hard work
and requires constant growth,
or it withers and dies.

### Woven into the Mundane

Spirituality is not other-worldly;
it is found in our relationships,
work, attitudes, illness, and dreams.
Simply put, spirituality is rooted in
ordinary emotional, physical, and mental life.
The difficulty lies in achieving
the concentrated attention needed
to observe what is going on,
moment by moment,
in ourselves and around us,
to uncover that spiritual dimension.

Spiritual growth hinges on our ability to see
the divine woven into mundane human reality . . .
a feat which will take a lifetime.

God humbly came to the earth He created.

The Cross is a symbol
of God's humility,
poverty, and love.

God's love lacks nothing
and nothing is held back.


## Wings

The hunger for God is insatiable.
The more the soul glimpses of God,
the greater the hunger for God.

To be in love is to be attentive to the object
of your love.
Which is why contemplation is vital
if you love God.

Contemplation and compassion
are the wings of Christian life.

The Christian life is composed
of four essential elements:
prayer, community, service, and study.

## *An Unlikely Partnership*

God seems to enjoy choosing the weak
to do His work.

God wants to be in partnership with us
and the partnership is formed in prayer.

Nothing in our lives is inconsequential to God.

Through Christ, with Christ, and in Christ
give glory to God.


## *Truly Listening*

To listen effectively to God
—or even to another human being—
one needs to be silent and attentive.

If we are truly listening to God or another,
truly paying attention,
there will be no hint of self-reflective consciousness—
there will only be silent receptivity.
To listen is to be silent.

The primary focus of prayer
is to lead the mind to stillness.

I need to spend less time trying to understand God
and more time adoring God.

### *An Act of Humility*

Prayer helps restore our awareness of God.

Prayer is an act of humility,
stemming from a mindfulness
of our inadequacy.

Prayer and humility go hand in hand:
prayer deepens humility
and humility deepens prayer.

Humility is the surest way to temper anger.

The mouth is very powerful:
it can heal and it can destroy.
Use it wisely.

### *The Mystical Ladder*

Only God knows who I am,
originally, essentially.
The Good News is God wants
to tell me who I am,
and what I can be.
Right now, God is busy
trying to teach me how to listen.
Truly listen.

Some degree of mysticism
is within the reach of everyone,
and all Christians should aspire to climb
as high as they can on the mystical ladder.

### The Best

Theological theses are useless
unless they live in our hearts.

Feelings of superiority over other
races, religions, and classes
begin with a refusal to listen to others
and end in acts of injustice.

Our spiritual life cannot afford to be elitist.

Authentic spirituality rejects separation
and embraces harmony.

God loves indiscriminately.
Such love is an impossibility for us.

### Crazy?

God's love manifested itself
in Christ's poverty and humility.

Submit to God the imperfections of your self-love.

Choose to let go of your life . . . to give it away.
Crazy?
Jesus did not think so.

Poverty brings you closer to Christ.

### Worry

Worrying about tomorrow destroys today.

Worry is a misuse of the gift of imagination.

Problems are opportunities to trust God for a solution.
With God, problems are transformed into blessings.

### Hidden Thoughts

All of humanity is intimately connected.
My most hidden thought affects
someone somewhere.

We all stand in constant need of one another.

The body of Christ is
the whole of humanity.

Everything you do
has eternal consequences.

### Thank You

If you want to show gratitude to God,
be generous toward others.

Where do you draw the line on altruism?

Jesus came to liberate not oppress.
Can I do anything other than what He did?

Charity is the supreme law of Christ.

Not caring about others
is the same thing as
not caring about yourself
. . . or Christ.

God does not take away suffering.
God asks us to enter into
the suffering of the other.
Jesus entered into
the suffering of human nature.

### *True Delights*

Nothing seen can compare
to the unseen glory
of the risen Lord.

God's love and mercy are my true delights.

The more I know about myself
the easier it is to be humble.

God's love for me is infinitely stronger
than my love for God will ever be.

### *The Center of the Universe*

We want to re-create creation
into our image and likeness.
We think we are the center
of the universe.

Christ is the center
of the universe.

### *A Life of Love*

God has chosen to be vulnerable and defenseless.
Jesus was as helpless as we are,
for he was "like us in all things but sin."
He was unprotected and unprivileged.

The life of Christ was a life of
love, surrender, and forgiveness.

You must renounce your own self-importance
to reach God.

God calls everyone to detachment and involvement
without one negating the other.

**129**

### The Answer

Whatever the question, Christ is the answer,
for He reveals the truth of the human condition
and the divine response.

After encountering Christ, two things will happen:
you will change and your world will change.

### Living with Contradiction

To live the Gospel forces us
to live with contradiction;
for the Gospel requires
a faith that believes
that when one has nothing,
one has everything.
Moreover, it asks us
to count poverty as riches
and humiliation as an honor.
It asks us to
dismiss the delights of life
and embrace our daily trials.

### Goodness and Being

It is God's nature not to be self-contained.
God wants to share.
God is relational by nature.
Goodness and being are wedded in God.

God is not static;
God is dynamic.
God does not stay
within the lines.

## Blessed Are the Poor

Jesus was poor because he chose to be poor.
He divested himself of the richness of his divinity
in order to be in solidarity with the poverty
of our humanity.

Jesus said, "Blessed are the poor."
We say, "Hide the poor,"
because they make us uncomfortable.

The way we treat the poor and the weak
reflects our essential and guiding view of life;
but, more important, it is the way
Christ evaluates our lives.

Whenever I use the possessive words
"my" and "mine,"
I am separating myself from others and from God.
All that I am belongs to God.

As long as my attention
is turned away from God and toward myself,
true human development ceases.

The meek are the only ones strong enough
to break down the walls of fear
that separate people.
Fear is at the core
of all human conflict.

## *Matthew 25:31- 46*

Matthew's Gospel reminds us that to serve
Christ the King
is to serve the least of our sisters and brothers.
But Jesus is not merely suggesting
that we be charitable.
Hardly.
Jesus is asking us to abandon our love of self
and to embrace our own
weakness and vulnerability.
Jesus is saying we cannot enter into
the universe of God
without relinquishing everything that binds us
to the false security
of our own imagined self-sufficiency.
God demands absolute allegiance.
Jesus is asking us to give ourselves
entirely over to him every day of our lives.
And this we find terrifying.

Helping the poor should not be a matter of
"I gotta give back";
it should stem from love, not guilt.

Love is a limitless self-emptying,
an on-going crucifixion
where we die to ourselves
in order to give ourselves
to the One
who is greater than ourselves.
We learn to love the One
by loving others.

## A Monet Painting

Think about a painting by Monet.
If you were to get very close to it,
you would see only random daubs of paint,
imperfect-looking individual brushstrokes.
Yet when you step back from the canvas,
you see fields of beautiful flowers.
Everyone on earth,
a vast assortment of people,
people of different faiths, different denominations,
are like those imperfect brushstrokes
of a Monet painting.

The essence of a Monet painting is its organization,
the combination of hundreds of individual strokes
of paint
working in harmony to create something beautiful.
And that is what we are called to do:
to work in harmony to bring
hope and healing to those who are suffering
from the cruel effects of chronic, unjust poverty.
At the foundation of all our different faiths
is compassion.
We show our love for God by how we treat
the least of God's children, no matter their faith.

And this involves more than giving our spare change.
We need to go out and embrace
the anawim in our midst,
the poorest of the poor,
those completely overwhelmed by want,
without voice or rights
in their surrounding community.

The Jewish Scriptures makes it abundantly clear
that to forget the anawim,
is to forget God.

And Jesus made care for the anawim
a litmus test for our love of God.

Elie Wiesel said:
"When someone suffers,
and it is not you, they come first.
Their suffering gives them priority.
To watch over another who grieves
is more urgent than to think about God."

### The Cries of the Poor

We need more than an emotional response
to the plight of the poor,
we need more than feelings of
sorrow and regret.
We need to be moved
by grace
to action.

When we hear
the cries of the oppressed,
the cries of the poor,
we hear
the voice of God.

Where there is weakness,
there is God.

We need to ask God
to shatter our complacency,
to strip us of our need
for comfort.

## St. Francis of Assisi

St. Francis of Assisi said,
"We must be simple, humble, and pure."
Sound advice.

Creation is wounded,
and St. Francis of Assisi asks us to be healers.

For St. Francis of Assisi,
the essential ingredient of Gospel poverty
is "living without grasping."
For most of us today,
our lives are marked by a hunger
to grab all we can.

## Hidden and Visible

Every day I experience God
both as distant and near,
both hidden and visible.

Each day presents me with opportunities
to grow in awareness of God's presence.

The door to God opens every day.
Each day I must enter the door.
And wait.
The cumulative effect
of entering and waiting
allows God
to enter and animate
God's presence within me.

# Small Drops of Love

*Mother Teresa said: "We cannot do great things in this world; we can only do small things with great love." She urged us to be "faithful in small things because it is in them that your strength lies . . . Do not think that love, in order to be genuine, has to be extraordinary. What we need is to love without getting tired." What she was saying is that the formula for becoming more fully united with God is to love, beginning with small acts of love which will not exhaust us, and that the easiest way to do this is by concentrating on the small, everyday things of our daily life and being open to manifesting small acts of love with every person and in every situation we encounter. In time, our small acts of love will increase, both in number and size, as love becomes more self-emptying and more inclusive.*

*Mother Teresa told her sisters that performing one small act of loving after another begins to make a difference. "How does a lamp burn?" she asks. "Through the continuous input of small drops of oil . . . My daughters, what are these drops of oil in our lamps? They are the small things of daily life: faithfulness, punctuality, small words of kindness, a thought for others, our way of being silent, of looking, of speaking, and of acting. These are the true drops of love."*

*Each of us can bring Light into the world through our tiny but continuous drops of love. There is no other way for the darkness to be defeated.*

# PART SIX

# Vespers

"Prayer was likewise a safeguard to this man [Francis of Assisi] of action who, rather than rely on his own efforts in everything he undertook, would ask in persevering prayer to be guided by the blessed Jesus. By every possible means he would urge his brothers to be earnest in prayer.

He was so constant himself in giving time to prayer that, whether walking, sitting down, working or resting, indoors or outside, he seemed to be always praying. It was as though he had dedicated to holy prayer, not only heart and body, but every piece of his activity and time."

From *The Tree of the Crucified Life of Jesus*
—*Early Documents*, Volume III, page 181

# Making All Things New

The interior life is the beginning of eternal life. Heaven does not begin after we die. It starts here and now as we respond to God's grace by making all things new and creating paradise on earth. Today, sadly, many people seem to have forgotten or have dismissed heaven, thereby ignoring the idea of eternally living with God. We are so preoccupied with the surface of life, we do not pay attention to the divine call to enter more deeply into the silent streams of a God-energized life of the Spirit which transforms us into more loving and compassionate beings who see beauty in everything, who love the truth, who thirst for justice and who embrace and protect all of creation. We watch TV, we shop, we fight, we ignore the common good, we applaud the rich and the powerful, we snub the poor and the weak, and we rape the environment.

### Trinity

Heaven is not a place;
it is a state of being . . .
a state of being fully in tune
with the Trinity.

The delight of the Trinity
is to pour itself out into Oneness.

Prayer is the Trinity praying in us.

### God Is . . .

Do not try to define God.
God exists above and beyond
human comprehension.

The intellect has a devil of a time
trying to grasp things of the spirit.

The rational exercise of logic
does not yield spiritual insight.

Childlike faith is the dwelling place of God.

### Hiding in Creation

All of creation and every creature
reflects some aspect of God.

God hides
in the created order
of things.

Every creature is a word of God.
Creation is not a dead-end.

## *Embracing Creation*

Creation is a limited expression
of God's self-expression.

God embraces creation
and self-gives
to creation.

Water expresses God.
We pollute water.

Creation is brought into union
with the Divine
through Christ.

## *A Temporary Expedient*

Christianity lives in the heart, not the head.
The head is for doctrine.

Live for God.
Literally, explicitly, without shame.

There is a mystic within everyone.

Time is a temporary expedient.
God does not live in time. God lives now.

God created time
but is not confined by it.

## *Seekers*

Sin blocks life's flow.

The joy of repentance is that it lightens the burden
of the past and sets us free
to discover and perform our life's work.

I am a seeker because God is a seeker.
God is always seeking us.

The contradictions, inconsistencies, and
incompatibilities of life
do not have to be explained or denied;
they must simply be endured.

For the most part, the life of prayer
is lived in darkness.

Everything is God. Nothing else.

I am stunned by how often in my life
I have failed to see the difference between
what is real and what is superficial.

## *Mother Teresa and the Zen Master*

A Zen Master was asked, "What is the path?"
He answered, without hesitation,
"Everyday life is the path."
The mundane and commonplace events
of our everyday life
are where we discover God.

Mother Teresa said,
"You can and you must expect suffering."
None of us has any choice when it comes to pain.
Pain and suffering catch us all.
The only choice we have in the matter
is what we do with it.
Christ hopes we transform our pain,
that we go from the cross to the resurrection . . .
and that is the true path.

## *Little Bits of Colored Tile*

The face of God is so vast
it is faceless from our limited perspective.
The great fifteenth-century German mystic
Nicholas of Cusa said,
"Every face you encounter in life
is a face of the Faceless One."

We are all part of the infinite reality
that is the face of God,
each of us are like little bits of colored tile
in the vast mosaic that is the Divine face,
each of us a tiny part of the infinite reality
that is the face of God.

## The Presence of God

The essence of Christianity can be boiled down
to one salient characteristic:
continual growth in a personal relationship
with Christ.
And that growth is fueled by prayer.
And prayer has three basic elements:
speaking to God,
listening to God,
and resting in the presence of God.

The heart of prayer is genuine sharing.

Prayer is a pause that refreshes.

Prayer is not a private affair,
not something to which we selfishly cling.
Prayer leads us out of ourselves
and into solidarity with the whole human family
and all living creatures.

## A Sacrament of Self-Giving

Christ gives me what I need
by taking away from me
everything I don't need.

Christ is not asking us merely to share
what we have;
He wants us to share what we are.
Giving of ourselves frees us to give what we have.

Jesus wants us to follow His example
and to face the cross.
He asks us to stand side-by-side
with those who are suffering.

He asks us to become Eucharist
for the hungry of the world.

Christ desires that we become
a sacrament of self-giving.

When we are weak,
Christ is strong.

## *Forgiven*

As Christians, we are penitents, but not guilt-ridden.
We are sinners, but we are forgiven.

Feeling negative about yourself
is not pleasing to God.

Humility is truth.
We know we are sinners;
we know we are forgiven.

In our helplessness,
God can do anything.

## *Eyes Wide Shut*

Grace opens the door
to the possibility of change.

Sin is saying no to grace.

Sin closes my eyes to the truth.

Sin destroys love and causes separation.

Minor sins are far from trivial
because they pave the way to major sins.

### A Lamentation

When I think how much time
I have wasted in my life
talking and thinking about
the imperfections of others,
it makes me sick.
So many lost opportunities
to be more like Christ,
extending goodwill and affection.

### Never Forgotten

Nothing you do can derail
God's love.

Sin, no matter how grievous, cannot destroy
God's love.

From God's perspective,
I am not needed . . .
I am simply loved.
And no matter what I do,
God never forgets me
or stops loving me.
Or you.

There is no corner of human existence
in which God does not want to be with us,
sharing our experience
of suffering and alienation.

God entered the human experience completely
in Jesus . . .
even the experience of the poor and suffering.

God wants your experience.

146

## *The Garden of Eden*

The purpose of Lent is to return to paradise,
to be made new.
During Lent, we head back to the garden,
we attempt to restore Eden.

Establish Eden wherever you go.

Perhaps the world's religions
should be more concerned
about the future of the world
rather than about getting
to another world in the future.

## *Spring Cleaning*

Lent is a spiritual journey
whose destination is Easter.

Because of our weakness,
we all too often—and too easily—betray
the gift of new life.
Lent helps us turn away from
our daily busyness and preoccupations,
helps us turn away from
our relentless search for material goods,
security, and pleasure.
Lent helps us strengthen and refocus our lives,
helps us taste again the sweetness
of our new life in Christ.

Lent is a time of spiritual spring cleaning.

Lent helps us escape the prison of this world.
Lent liberates us from the chains of sin.

The simple reality of our humanity
is that we follow our desires.
Lent helps us identify the desires
which direct our lives.
During Lent, we slowly come to realize
where our treasure is,
where our heart is.
Lent connects us to our deepest desire,
the hunger and thirst for the Absolute
which is buried in the core of our being.

Passion for anything other than God
is a useless passion.

### Keep Planting

In God's eyes
whether or not we are successful
is unimportant.
What is important to God
is that we are faithful.
We must keep planting
and leave the rest to God.

My primary struggle in life
is the struggle between my nature
(which strives to put me first)
and God's grace
(which prompts me to put you first).

For my life to be genuinely authentic,
the essence of my interior being
must be manifested in my external life,
in my daily actions.

I need to be who I am.

## Nothing Less Than Everything

The cost of following Jesus is
nothing less than everything:
one must abandon self
in order to imitate
the self-transcendence
of the Cross and Resurrection.

The Cross symbolizes the extremity of helplessness
more than the extremity of suffering.
The Cross rejects power and accepts surrender.

We love power more than people.

When we have little or no worldly power to rely on,
we are able to offer unambiguous love and service.

## Radically Vulnerable

On the Cross, through Jesus,
God became radically vulnerable
to the point of death.

Love means radically traveling
as far as Christ did . . . to the point
of suffering and death.

We don't like giving ourselves totally . . .
we only give up to a certain point.

Suffering and love go together.
Love eventually hurts
and it hurts to love.
But love we must.

Christ loved to the point
where there was nothing
left to give.

This total self-emptying love
led to a new life,
led to the resurrection.

Love defeats death.


### Running from Reality

All acts of charity are essentially acts of obedience—
that is, we are doing what God wants us to do:
share His love and mercy.

To confuse appetite with love is a huge mistake.

Love and sacrifice are handmaidens.

To run from pain is to run from reality.


### I Forgive You

Arms full of resentment
are not capable of embracing God . . .
or each other.

My enemies are the best people
to teach and help me practice compassion.

Forgive, forgive, forgive, forgive, forgive.


### One Word

God is talking to us.
God has always been talking to us.
God will always be talking to us.

God has been, is, and will be saying
one word: Love.

And in that love
rests a profound truth:
We are one.
We just imagine
(as Thomas Merton pointed out)
that we are not one,
that division exists within
the human family.

In God there is unity.
In the beginning,
we were one.
We are still one.
We just need to recover
our original unity.

## One

Christ loved every human being,
without exception,
without limits.
Can we do otherwise?

Love casts out the darkness
of hate and division.
From love
flows understanding, compassion,
mercy, forgiveness,
and peace.
Love unites.
Love is One.

## *The Unity of Life*

There is the voice of God
and the echo of the voice of God.
Hearing the difference
between the two is important.
The difference is the same as the difference
between a being and an image of a being.

Be alert to the relentless unity of life.

When it comes to prayer,
sincerity is more important than the quantity
—or even the quality.

Truth guides you to integrity,
which is completeness.
But truth without love is pointless.

Happiness is being satisfied
with what you have.

Do not measure yourself against others.


## *Gotta Minute, God?*

Prayer is the natural expression of the friendship
that exists between myself and God,
a friendship initiated in love by God.

A free moment is a moment free
to speak to God.

The post office is a great place
to have a long chat with God.
Praise God for long lines.

## *Where Hope Abounds*

In the sea of dysfunction and destruction
that engulfs so much of modern life,
there is an island where hope abounds,
a sacred space that nurtures the soul.
That island has a name: prayer.
Intimacy with God grows freely on this island.

When freed from merely mouthing petitions,
prayer expands our self-knowledge and
consciousness.


## *Unruffled Calmness*

Prayer helps us flee from the storm
of inner thoughts
and the noise that engulfs modern life.

To neglect prayer is to neglect God.

Prayer creates the unruffled calmness
required to encounter God.

We say we never hear
God's voice.
A Desert Father explains why,
simply and clearly:
"God is heard by those
who are listening."
It is hard to listen
when we are always
moving and talking,
always busy doing
important stuff.
Stop. Sit. Listen. Hear.

### Flip Sides of a Coin

Action is as important as prayer;
each of us must take responsibility
for meeting the world's need,
for we are the accomplices of evil
if we do nothing to prevent it.

Contemplation and action
are flip sides of the same coin.

Contemplation means to witness and respond.


### Love Made Visible

Suffering, along with failure, is universal,
an inescapable fact of human life.
But compassion, silence, and hope
gives us a way through the suffering.

The healing of the world
begins within us . . .
and yet can never end with us.

The best way to love God
is to relieve the pain and suffering of others.

When we relieve the pain and suffering of others,
we make God's love visible.

Compassion without works of mercy
was inconceivable to Jesus.


### Goodness and Humility

Christ is the total gift of goodness.

The death of Jesus
materialized
the humility of God.

You cannot worship God
and dominate others.

We must always make space
for the other.

Our job is to become vessels
of love and compassion,
like the poor and humble
God we seek.

### Revolutionary Love

During his life,
Christ was unwavering
in his resistance
to everything
that denied or rejected
God's unending,
non-violent love.

Christ's life was marked
by bold acts
of civil disobedience
against every injustice
He encountered.

Christ gave his life fully to God
and God's passion for justice and mercy.
The life of Christ
was a life of
revolutionary love.

Christ came to offer
a communion of love
to every human being.

**155**

## Christ's Friends

If you are poor or needy,
if you are despised by all,
if you are a sinner,
then Christ considers you to be his friend
and he welcomes you to his banquet table.

If you are looking for Jesus,
you'll find Him in the midst of those
who are being crucified, rejected,
alienated, and oppressed.
He is in the dark corners of your neighborhood,
waiting for you to help Him.
Unless we stand shoulder to shoulder
with the poorest of the poor,
we will not find the crucified Christ,
nor experience the richness of His resurrection.

## Creating a Better Society

Christ is revealed
in every embrace of the poor.

The richer you are,
the less need you have
to interact with others.

Poverty has the power to crush the human spirit.

Creativity is God's gift to every human being.
Creating a better society is the noblest form
of creativity.

### Bread and Wine

True poverty is total trust in God.

No human life is meaningless to or forgotten by God.

Within the frailty of our humanity,
the majesty of God resides.

God reveals himself in simplicity,
in the simplicity of prayer
and the simplicity of bread and wine.

### Holy and Whole

Following your deepest aspirations
makes life meaningful.

Poverty of spirit frees us
from the tyranny of wealth.

Littleness is a big part of holiness.

Holiness is wholeness.

### The Plague of Consumerism

Relinquishing the possessions of the ego
we all amass inside ourselves
is the most demanding form of poverty.

Simplicity immunizes you from the plague
of consumerism.

Through simplicity we learn that self-denial
paradoxically leads to true self-fulfillment.
Simplicity allows us to hold the interests
of others above our self-interest.
Real simplicity is true freedom.

## A Different Point of View

At its root, there is only one reason
for the existence of poverty:
selfishness, which is a manifestation of
a lack of authentic love.

Sadly, we tend to think of the homeless
as social nuisances.
Jesus had a different point of view
and suggested that the poor
are pathways to God.

By serving the poor
we are not only practicing Christian charity,
we are also reforming ourselves.

We don't have to solve
all the problems for the poor;
just being with them
goes a long way toward
lightening their burden.

## Fully Alive

God loves me because
I am weak and powerless,
not in spite of those qualities.
I am poor and needy,
and God lifts me up.

Without self-denial and sacrifice,
my prayer life will wither on the vine.

Poverty of spirit is a means
of maintaining a continual attitude
of dying to self

without succumbing
to self-hatred or causing a lack of self-esteem.
We need to die to self
because it is the only way
to be fully alive to God.


## An Empty Vessel

Joy is never found in possessing.

Sex, power, fame, and money
are not enough
to still the longing within us.
Only God is enough.

God can't pour love into a vessel
that is already full.

A cluttered heart is a deaf heart.

When your emotions and desires
are moderate
it is easier to reach a state of harmony
within yourself and with others.


## False Idols

Poverty of spirit is a manger of gentle receptivity
which allows the Divine to be born within us.
To be wholly present to God,
with all of our heart, mind, and soul,
we must be poor in spirit.

Poverty of spirit is far more than material poverty.
While material poverty may help

to facilitate poverty of spirit,
it is nonetheless important to realize
that a person without possessions
can still be possessed
by a craving for things.

It is the craving that makes us restless,
distracting our hearts and minds
from being present to God alone.
Poverty of spirit frees us from being
divided by false idols and uncurbed passions.

### A Miracle

Jesus said he was meek and humble of heart.
What am I?

Humility is a miracle.

Through my own strength,
I can accomplish nothing.

Abandon your ego and enter heaven.

### A Supreme Act of Humility

St. Francis of Assisi saw God as humble
because God is always inclined
toward another.
In the Trinity, Francis saw goodness
giving itself away,
completely and inexhaustibly.

God, who has no limits, chose
to take on the limitations
of a material being.
In doing so, God had to have
his diapers changed.
Taking on our limitations
was a supreme act of humility.


## Organic Living

Our souls are transformed
in the furnace of self-forgetfulness.

We can become holy to the extent
that we cease to live
and Christ lives in us.

Surrendering ourselves to God's glory
and glorifying God through service to others
is the most organic way
of transforming our lives and spirits.


## A Question before Bed

At the end of the day,
pause and reflect on this question:
Was my life today a living sign
of the presence of God to others?

# The Movement of Grace

*Isn't it odd that we pray "Thy kingdom come" yet we really love and cling to this world and its fleeting pleasures? Isn't it odd that we pray "Thy will be done" yet we cultivate and worship our own self-will?*

*I need to strive continually to make Christ present in every ambit of my life, in every encounter, every deed, every relationship. Of course, I all too frequently shut the door on Christ, or worse set up a wall around some hidden area of my being that I want to keep all to myself. It's crazy how we seem to protect the very things or behaviors we should reject. The fact is we pray . . . and we sin. But where there is sin, there too is grace, overflowing and abundant. But only in stillness can we see the movement of grace.*

*My faith may be fickle at times, but God is always faithful.*

*Alleluia. Alleluia. Alleluia.*

# PART SEVEN

# Compline

## The Praises of God

You are holy Lord God Who does wonderful things.

You are strong. You are great. You are most high.
You are the almighty king. You holy Father,
King of heaven and earth.

You are three and one, the Lord God of gods;
You are the good, all good, the highest good,
Lord God loving and true.

You are love, charity; You are wisdom, You are humility,
You are patience, You are beauty, You are meekness,
You are security. You are rest,
You are gladness and joy, You are our hope, You are justice,
You are moderation, You are all our riches to sufficiency.

You are beauty, You are meekness,
You are the protector, You are our custodian and defender,
You are strength, You are refreshment. You are our hope,
You are our faith, You are our charity,
You are all our sweetness, You are our eternal life:
Great and wonderful Lord, Almighty God, Merciful Savior.

St. Francis of Assisi
—*Early Documents*, Volume I, page 109

# Perfect Love

*St. Thérèse of Lisieux said, "My vocation is to love." That is our vocation too, our daily vocation. Only love will put you on the path to sanctity. Only love will get you to heaven. And your love must include the people who are marginalized, the people who are homeless, the people who are dirty and who smell, the people who are addicted, the people who are imprisoned and the people who live in the squalor of developing nations. Love must go way beyond ourselves and our family and friends. It must go to all those whom everyone else rejects or excludes. No one should be outside the perimeter of our love.*

*This is the only thing that matters: that you have love for one another.*

*If love is absent from your life, Christ is absent from your life. If you deny your love to someone, you deny your love to Christ. That is how radical the Gospel is.*

*The Eucharist compels us to become what we have received: Perfect Love.*

### Compassion Antidote

Prayer is the consciousness
of God's loving presence.

Contemplation without compassion is useless.

Compassion is the only antidote to the plague
of greed and violence
that threatens to destroy us.

Compassion is far removed from pity.
Compassion grows from an awareness
of our shared weakness.

To be compassionate requires the letting go
of our egos and problems,
and entering into the suffering of another.

Compassion fosters a spirit of togetherness.

Compassion for others is the surest way
to transcend our own sinfulness.

## Winners and Losers

In today's society, competition is far removed
from healthy ambition
and has become highly neurotic and aggressive.

Competition suffocates compassion.

Competition divides us into camps
of winners and losers,
and fosters a spirit
of separateness and hostility.
Compassion's fruit is unification,
as it gives birth to togetherness and mutuality.

Charity is the best cure for loneliness.

When I feel like a failure,
when I feel ineffectual,
when I feel a deep sense of shame,
I then begin to feel more intensely
the scandal of the Cross
and the defeat and death of Jesus.

## Fueled by Love

Competition seeks to defeat our opponents;
compassion longs to embrace the defeated.

Competition is driven by compulsion;
compassion is fueled by love.

Compulsions are nurtured
in the soil of self-centeredness.

Self-centeredness blinds one
to the needs and feelings of others.

Without compassion there is nothing to stop
the compulsion to destroy one another.

## *Either/Or*

Contemplation and solitude increase our ability
to become more compassionate.

Compassion frees us from
the "either/or" dualism that chokes us,
and leads us to a reconciliation of opposites.

As we grow in compassion,
we see more clearly how the world
is interconnected.

Compassion opens the door to heaven.

What happens to a poor person
living in the slums of Nairobi, Kenya,
is happening to you.
We are one.
Compulsion, competition, and dualism
deny that unity.

## *The Way of the Cross*

Christ's suffering and death on the cross
led to his resurrection.

When we become one with Jesus forsaken
in the suffering of others
we both experience ourselves
passing through the cross
with Christ
into the resurrection life
of Trinitarian love and unity.

When we embark on the way of the cross,
we travel through suffering
and discover the Love
that is God within us.

## The Sacred Heart

The sweet, gentle, merciful, always-loving
Heart of Jesus
beckons us to join our heart with His,
to fully join in His incarnation,
passion, death, and resurrection
on a daily basis,
opening our hearts to deeper levels
of love, humility, evangelical poverty,
compassion, and unselfish service to others
so that we may one day enter
into full unity with God.

O Most Sacred Heart of Jesus,
so often broken by my sinfulness,
have mercy on me
and draw me closer to You today.

## The Latest Fad

Compassion is equally as important as worship
and liturgy.

Pity is far removed from compassion.
Pity grows out of a sense of superiority
rather than a spirit of solidarity with others.

Compassion requires us to forget ourselves
and remember others.
Which is why we see so little of it,
even among Christians.
We don't want to die to ourselves.

Spiritual transformation is far removed
from the latest fad for self-improvement.

We can improve ourselves
but only God can transform us.
Transformation involves a total metamorphosis.
To be transformed requires death and rebirth.

## Holy and Divine

For Jesus, compassion was a way of life,
and he repeatedly and strongly urged
his followers to be compassionate.

Jesus said,
"Be compassionate as your Father is compassionate."

Compassion teaches us to treat all creation
as holy and divine.

Everything that lives is part of one infinite,
gracious Spirit.

God is present
in the slap of the sea
against the shore.

## The Shadow of the Cross

Life is discovered in its interruptions.

Pleasure is a gift from God.
The problem is we have turned
pleasure into a god.

When I am tired,
temptations are wide awake.

All joy is fleeting,
living always in the shadow of the Cross.

### *You Win by Losing*

Seek to find in every man and woman
your brother and sister.
Doing so, is the only way
to escape sin and find salvation.

We often hear the Cross preached,
but we rarely see the Cross lived.

All our lives, society has taught us that life
at its core is a competition,
and we need to be constantly struggling to win.
Christ teaches us something very different:
life is really all about love,
tenderness, mutuality . . . and moreover,
you win by losing!

Finding Christ is easy:
visit the poor, the suffering, the sick, and the dying.
Jesus is there with them,
offering His abiding love.

### *Wounded*

Whenever I am tempted to feel proud,
I try to think about the humility of Christ.

God took on human form
and was willing to be wounded,
to suffer for us.

The love of Christ desires
only to serve.

Christ is truly present in all acts
of compassion.

### Not Optional

Christianity leads to the Cross,
and it doesn't offer an easy way around it.

I need to become more and more intimate
with the poor and crucified Christ.

We have forgotten the Cross.
But the crucifixion of Christ
cannot be reversed.
Paradise has been paved over;
happiness on earth is impossible—
without the cross, without God.

For Christians, the Cross is not optional—
we must accept it.

Without the Cross there is no Resurrection.

By avoiding the Cross, you avoid entering
into the central mystery and message of Christ.

God wants us to become uncomfortable—
so we become more open to change.

### The Cries of God

We pray for our daily bread.
Yet for millions of people around the world,
their daily bread consists of
violence, famine, and destruction.
Did God hear our prayer and not theirs?
No.
God hears the cries of the poor.
We do not hear the cries of God
asking us to be divine hands
tending to the needs of the poor.
God took on human form

as a vulnerable baby,
the child of homeless refugees,
needing human help
in the ongoing work of creation.
We are God's messengers
delivering food and hope
to those living with hunger and death.

### The Tin Man and Me

In the presence of God, my sins are magnified.

Embrace the Tin Man,
the Straw Man, and the frightened Lion
within you.

Violence is in the human heart.

If we don't acknowledge our own evil,
we end up projecting it onto others.

Look into your heart of darkness.

We must process our own inner potential for evil.

The strain of evil (and love) runs through everything.

### Here Comes the Judge

Judging others is fun!
What?
Yes, fun, because it distracts me
from looking at and dealing with my own sins . . .
which is not fun.

Neither praise nor blame should disturb
my inner equilibrium.

Nine times out of ten, anger is a misspent emotion.

## *Hello, World*

Do not renounce the world.
Only renounce evil in the world
and everything within yourself
that hinders your spiritual life and growth.

Evil is repelled by virtue.

If you are not aware of your sinfulness,
you will never find a cure for your addiction to sin.

The soul is purified by love and self-control.

## *A Long Way To Go*

My doubts about God arise from my sinfulness.
Sin disrupts union with God.
When I turn away from sin
and restore my spiritual union with God,
all my doubts about God's existence and love
or Christ's divinity dissolve and float away.

I pretend my intellect is detached
from worldly allurements,
but my attraction to sensual pleasures
proves I have a long way to go
in order to reach my goal
of living for God alone.

## Out of Fashion

Do not allow actions and attitudes
to be governed
by merely subjective moods and feelings.

The bondage of selfishness
prevents us from living
in generous communion with others,
in friendship and love.

As long as our attention is turned away
from God and toward ourselves,
authentic human development ceases.

To chase after self-fulfillment
is to be led into a spiritual desert
and a life of impoverishment and hunger.

The Gospel asks us to turn from a life of
tepidity, indolence, and self-centeredness
and strive for spiritual alertness,
self-giving generosity,
and loving abandonment to the will of God.

Long to transcend the fluctuations
of time and fashion.
Seek eternal and unchanging truths.

Find yourself in giving yourself.

The glorification of God
should be the primary focus of our life.

## Betrayal

Why do I so often choose
the transitory and corruptible
over the eternal and everlasting?

When our hearts are devoted to anything but God,
we betray not only God
but also ourselves.

## Wind Catchers

Dryness in prayer forces me
to identify with the abandoned Jesus.

I am poor, needy, and helpless—thank God!

Prayer is hard because it demands
honesty before God.

Contemplation forces me to identify
and confront the pathologies of my spiritual life,
most of which stem from my refusal
to know and love myself as a creature.

The gentle winds of grace are always blowing.
We need to become wind catchers.
Prayer is our net.

Your prayer life will become greener
the more often you water it.

### Armor of Silence

To be fruitful, Christian action
should be preceded by contemplation.

Contemplation frees us from self-serving
and prepares us to lead a life of service
to others without unconsciously desiring
our own success.

Contemplation cultivates a spirit of receptivity
and a listening heart.

Put on the armor of silence.

### Movement in Stillness

In meditation, when the image disappears,
time ceases.

Thought, with its love of comparisons,
often breeds dishonesty.
Meditation is the freeing of the mind
from all dishonesty.

Imagination and thought have no place in
meditation.

Meditation is emptying the mind of the known.

Meditation is movement in stillness.

Quiet the brain, still the mind, move into
meditation.

## *Jumping-Jack*

Desires are endless.

Nurture attentiveness and awareness.

To enter fully into silence,
we need to drop all preoccupations,
being awake only to the presence of the moment.

Our fears, our anxieties, our desires,
and our jumping-jack thoughts
hinder us from experiencing
the joy and beauty of the present moment.

Love and fear cannot be roommates.
Love will drive out fear
or fear will drive out love.

## *A First Step*

To accept life's uncertainties
is a first step to living in peace.

Serenity follows surrender.

## *Going Nowhere*

Apart from God there is no direction,
just circular reasoning going nowhere.

The best time to pray
is when you don't feel like praying,
because that is when you most need to pray.

### Are We Having Fun Yet?

Our active lives need the counterbalance
of contemplative prayer.
Prayer is not optional.

Most days I don't feel like praying.
Prayer is not fun;
worse, frequently it is boring.
Besides, we have more important things to do.
So, it is easy to ignore prayer.
Which is why prayer needs
to be willed and practiced.
Determination and routine are essential
to developing a healthy and vibrant prayer life.

Prayer is a serious duty.
We need to come to our prayer time
composed and concentrated.
We must drop our desires and goals,
our inner clamoring and focus our attention
on the task at hand:
to become present and still . . .
and ready to pray.

Prayer is love, the seeking to be one
with the object of our desire.

Without prayer, faith weakens
and the spiritual life withers and dies.

Faith gives birth to prayer
and needs prayer to sustain itself.

Prayer is as important to faith
as our next breath is to our lives.

It is our inner life that gives
stability and direction to our lives.

## *A Waste of Time*

Prayer is the consciousness
of God's loving presence.

The closer you come to God
the more compassion you will have
for your neighbor.

If the fruit of our contemplation
is not an increased love of others,
then our contemplation is faulty
and a waste of time.

Spirituality and social responsibility are
interwoven.

Jesus understood that compassion
had to be far more than a feeling.
For Jesus, compassion
was never separated from action.

## *The Cornerstone*

All too often we more readily cater
to the needs of our bodies
than to our soul.

Stillness stills unruly passions.

Contemplation quiets our restless,
relentless quest for sensual pleasure.

The cornerstone of the spiritual life consists of:
stillness, prayer, love, and self-control.

## A Thin Line

The line between happiness and depression
is very thin.
Prayer broadens it.

Without solitude,
finding sanity and sanctity
is virtually impossible.

Time alone is a doorway
to yourself . . . and God.

Silence is not emptiness;
silence is a presence.

## The Bread of Life

In a humble loaf of bread
God proclaims God's bountiful love.

We search for food that perishes
while the bread of life
goes untouched.

The food we give to a hungry person
is a mundane sign of divine love.

Feed your hungry soul
in the solitude of prayer.

## *Bad Choice*

Christ asks us to renounce
comfort and security.
Our culture teaches us to seek
comfort and security.
We seem to have chosen our culture
over our Lord.

Freeing yourself from material things is easy.
Much harder is freeing yourself from thoughts
about them.

The pull of possessions is overcome by sharing . . .
joyfully.

Christ asks us to renounce all that we possess,
and all that possesses us.

## *When We Are Nothing*

We always hold something back,
always save something for ourselves,
always save a piece of ourselves.
Jesus says we need to give ourselves away,
to empty ourselves completely.
It seems impossible. It is impossible.
Only with and through Jesus
is self-emptying possible.
But the cost is enormous.
It costs everything to become nothing.
But when we are nothing,
then we are everything to Jesus.

## *Money*

Our love of pleasure, praise, possessions,
and money
is a breeding ground for every evil.

Humility and self-control are able to defuse
our passion for pleasure, praise, and riches.

There is nothing wrong with money—
as long as it is shared.

Generosity is a sign of wisdom.


## *Stuff*

If we do not move
beyond the materialism
that permeates our society
we will be doomed
to a life of
spiritual deprivation.

Stuff is not
the stuff of life.

In the darkness of our day
we must be beacons
of God's light.

We reach the summit of spirituality
when we are able
to unify mystical theology
with prophetic ethics.

### Shut Up and Sit Down

Quiet talkativeness

Still busyness.

The superfluous distracts us
from the supernatural.

### Good Enough

Sometimes I look in the mirror
and do not like what I see.
Imperfections, weaknesses, deficiencies.
At times, who I am may not be good enough
for my family and friends,
may not even be good enough for myself,
but it is always good enough for God.

Mercifully, God accepts me as I am,
where I am,
and never requires that I resolve
all the confusions, conflicts, and contradictions
that churn within me
before I am acceptable to Him.

### My Agenda

God gave us life.
To give our life back to God
is to enter into the fullness of joy and peace.

This is life's biggest question:
Is my agenda God's agenda?

## *Doubts and Questions*

There are days when I question God's existence,
doubt the reality of God's love.
On those days, I must enter my weakness
and blindness,
and open my heart to God
and be filled with spiritual nourishment.
I must resist the habits of a lifetime,
which have conditioned me
to turn to destructive behavior
when I encounter fear and loneliness.

## *An Image of Love*

An icon of the Blessed Virgin Mary
presents us with an image of love,
as it reveals the victory of love.

Mary asked for nothing
and was given everything.

Mary's life illustrates and celebrates
God's faith in humanity.

## *A Road to Isolation*

The road to a deeper spiritual life
is also a road to isolation . . .
and rejection.
You will be seen as "odd"
by family, friends, and society.
You will be culturally out of tune.
You have changed . . .
are changing:
and that threatens the status quo,
hence the isolation and rejection.

Being aware that I am a solitary creature
in infinite space prompts me to see
the value of silence
as the most effective form
of attentiveness to God.

## *A Saint*

Worldly desires create worldly distress.

All human beings were created to live a holy life.

What is a saint?
Someone whose words and actions
are in complete harmony.

## *Intimate Communion*

Each of us is on a life-long journey to wholeness.
We all want to overcome the fractures and divisions
we feel within ourselves

and among our circle of family and friends.
Our lives are like puzzle parts
and we can't see the full picture.

Wholeness and completeness are ultimately
only found in intimacy with God.
And intimacy with God is only found
through desire and surrender.
When we desire God above all else
and when we let go of our clinging egos,
God is free to enter into intimate communion
with us.

## *A Good Neighbor*

The essential unity of God
is manifested in personal love,
which brings us into unity
with all humanity and creation.

God's love brings you into an ever deepening
communion with your neighbor.

Christian spirituality is rooted in communion,
a life shared with others in imitation of the Trinity.

A consciousness of God's presence in all of creation
empowers us to love our neighbor.

Holiness is social because it manifests itself
in kindness, compassion, and charity.

To walk with Jesus
is to walk in communion
with all people.

## Embracing Grace

The Cross transforms all pain,
sorrow, and affliction
into pathways to paradise.

As our troubles and struggles mount,
the gifts of grace flow more abundantly.

Every failure contains the grace to start anew.

We must embrace grace every day.
Amazing Grace

# Amazing Grace

*As I put the period at the end of the last sentence, my little dog—Gracie—jumped up onto my lap. I smiled and hugged her. Her formal name is Grace Noel. I rescued her from the pound on Christmas Eve, 2000.*

*Life had dealt Gracie a bad hand. During the first six months of her life, she had been abused and abandoned. She was afraid of everything. Her constant nervousness was manifested physically in a condition known as "involuntary urination." If you went near her, she quivered, lay down, rolled over and urinated. Gracie demanded unconditional love and unending patience. The day after Christmas, I was ready to return her to the pound. But her cute yet sad face would not allow me to do it.*

*She was as weak and fragile as I was. Little Gracie needed my love and patience as much as I needed God's love and patience.*

*In a womb of love, Gracie grew into a new dog. In time, the constant, uncontrollable urinating stopped. Her fearfulness was replaced by a jumping joyfulness. Likewise, in the womb of God's love, I was growing—albeit ever so slowly and far slower than Gracie—into a new man.*

*Gracie needed someone to stick with her, to give her time to forget the past and to feel at home. I stuck with Gracie, and she found a new life.*

*Because God is with me, I am able to find God. God's presence in my life draws me into a deeper adoration of God. It is a slow, cumulative process. Each day requires more of a response from me. I often fail. But adoration is a gift. Still, it demands time and patience. Waiting for God demands I have patience with myself, even more patience than I had to have with Gracie. Each day, I come to God . . . and wait. Slowly, in silence, day by day, as my awareness of God's presence grows within, I am being transformed. As my clinging selfishness is chipped away, my eyes are more able to see Christ in the weak, the hurting, and the hungry, and my heart is more willing to serve them.*

*But I have a long way to go. My ego still threatens to topple Christ from the throne of my life. My faults still far outnumber my virtues.*

*I am still very much a blind beggar . . . in constant need of God's love and patience.*

*And so I continue to stretch out open hands to the silence of God.*

## About the Author

Gerard Thomas Straub is a documentary filmmaker and an award-winning author of four books, including *The Sun and Moon Over Assisi* (awarded First Prize for Spirituality by the Catholic Press Association) and a photo/essay book on global poverty, *When Did I See You Hungry?*

Mr. Straub has written and directed thirteen documentary films, three of which have aired on many PBS television stations, including *We Have a Table for Four Ready,* which tells the story of a soup kitchen run by Franciscan friars in Philadelphia, and *Room Enough for Joy,* which tells the story of a L'Arche community in Tacoma, Washington, that serves the needs of twenty mentally disabled children and adults. Mr. Straub also had a long and distinguished career as a network television producer in New York and Hollywood, where he produced a number of dramatic television series including the wildly popular *General Hospital.*

Mr. Straub, who is a Secular Franciscan, is the founder and president of The San Damiano Foundation, which produces films that celebrate the spirituality of St. Francis of Assisi and the Franciscan concern for the poor, social justice, peace, non-violence, prayer, and the integrity of creation. The San Damiano Foundation has been written about in *The New York Times, Los Angeles Times, St. Petersburg Times, National Catholic Reporter* (cover story), *U.S. Catholic,* and *Sojourners* magazine, and has been featured in stories which have aired on *Religion and Ethics Newsweekly* (PBS), *Life & Times* (KCET-TV, the PBS station in Los Angeles), and *News Conference* (KNBC-TV News in Los Angeles). In 2003, the University of Dayton presented Mr. Straub with the Daniel J. Kane Religious Communications Award, an annual award given to a person who has made "an outstanding lifetime dedication to gospel values through various forms of media." He has been given honorary doctorate degrees from St. Bonaventure University and St. Francis University.

Mr. Straub lives in North Hollywood, California.

For further information about Mr. Straub and the work of the San Damiano Foundation, visit the website: www.San DamianoFoundation.org